The Smart
English in Japan

By Charlie Moritz and Martin Bragalone

Special thanks to **Diego Medrano** for the foreword and his contribution on University Teaching, and to **Thomas Paeme** and **Nicholas Susatyo** for sharing their stories.

Paperback cover background art by Polina Valentina, licensed through shutterstock.com

ISBN: 9781549607790

Published on Amazon via CreateSpace 2017

Contents

Who are we?

I'm Charlie, and I've been teaching English in Japan since 2012.

I have gone from working at a standard eikaiwa (with standard pay) to one of the world's most famous pre-schools, Fuji Kindergarten (featured in a TED Talk by the architect Takaharu Tezuka entitled "The best kindergarten you've ever seen"). I have spent years working out exactly how to get the best English teaching jobs with the lowest time investment but the highest rewards both financially and creatively. Now I work part-time as an English teacher while freelancing as a web developer and building my own businesses in Japan.

If you listen to the strategies we talk about, I'm sure you can find the same success and more!

I'm Martin, and I've been both a teacher in Japan and a Japanese-to-English translator.

I started my journey in Japan as an exchange student to a sleepy little town in Hokkaido during junior high school. I taught English in Japan for several years while I began to build my freelance Japanese translation portfolio. I have worked since then using Japanese language both as an in-house translator and freelance translator. No matter what you strive to achieve from your time in Japan, we are certain English teaching will offer you flexibility and infinite varieties of opportunities in Japan.

We started Live Work Play Japan in 2016 to help foreigners in Japan to have a great experience here. We believe that loving your time in Japan is about having a great living situation, fulfilling and high-paying work, and excitement in your free time.

Between us we have read hundreds of books about psychology, education, philosophy, Japanese language and business in order to put together the strategies that we talk about in this book. This isn't just a reference guide, we have both used these strategies to get incredibly high success rates at interviews for jobs in Japan. We have been writing since early 2016 to help foreigners in Japan get what they need to become high performing and in-demand members of the international community here.

If you apply what we are teaching in this book, you can get better jobs. You will have to go out there, work hard and use the techniques. If you don't try, you can't succeed.

Foreword

By Diego Medrano

While there are countless reasons people fail - some within our control and some that are not - there really is only one method by which people become successful:

Hard work, done well, with one eye looking down the road to the future.

When I first arrived to Japan, I knew next to nothing about the job market, career prospects, average salaries, or school reputations. Over the years I've made mistake after mistake, learning by doing and soliciting the advice of any kind veteran teacher willing to lend an ear. The internet age has opened the floodgates of information, both good and bad, and has encourage people to share their stories and advice. I have long seen a need for teaching professionals to have a source of solid, trustworthy advice given by real teachers successfully living and working in Japan.

That's why I was so excited when Live Work Play Japan asked me to be a part of this book. Since 2016, they have been providing actionable, high quality content to their unique tribe of professionally-minded individuals who believe in the incredible opportunities for success that are available in Japan. To help those individuals, this book contains advice and information from real teachers currently working in Japan, with the goal of turning a life of subsistence in an entry-level position into a high paying, highly respectable career.

Japan can be a difficult country to get a solid footing in. Of course culture and language will slow you down at first, but more importantly what you should realize is that you are effectively starting your life over again. Nobody knows you, you might have just finished university and have unproven skills, and you have a ticking time-bomb strapped to your back, your visa. The reality is, the barriers to entry for your competition in the job market are lower than ever. How do you compete in a new country where you might not speak the language?

You have to put yourself in the way of opportunities you are qualified to do well.

The old adage is true. It doesn't matter how early you arrive at your eikaiwa, how many overtime hours you put in vacuuming the floor and preparing games, or even, sadly, the amount of knowledge your students walk away with. **When it comes to your success, what matters is that you're working hard in the right direction, making the right moves to get to where you want to go.** Think carefully about the things your current employer will find good and impressive, but also the things your future employer will find good and impressive. What can you use as ammunition for that better job? This isn't to say you shouldn't vacuum the floor or prepare fun games, it's a good habit to have and shows you respect your work and your students, but what are you actually doing to benefit the school and yourself as a teacher? What can actually be converted into written proof of your ability to do a higher job?

In the same vein, if your colleagues and employers had to choose three adjectives to describe you, what do you think they would be?

Capable, educated and confident?

Driven, talented and popular with students?

Or would it be lazy, easily flustered and dull?

These are all decisions that you make as a teacher in Japan, to either do the bare minimum and show up just on time to not get in trouble, or do a remarkable job that will set you up for future success.

Many young professionals get caught up in the minimalistic eikaiwa/ALT lifestyle - with the quality of their work not being tested to its limit, and making just enough money to feed their fancies and indulge when possible. It doesn't have to be that way, and if you follow the advice in this book you can start making a change that will allow you to make more money, have more free time for holidays and gain the respect you deserve as a teacher.

We don't become experts overnight

We only gain professional confidence after experiencing success and failure in a hundred different scenarios a hundred different times. How can you expect to ever get a high paying, high benefits teaching position when you freeze up during a particularly bad teacher evaluation? How can you move on in your career if you're self-conscious in front of the classroom, or if you lose your temper at the slightest challenge to authority? Are you able to handle a question that you don't know the answer to, or, if you do know the answer and the students aren't getting it, can you recognize that and pull back, start over again with a new approach?

I often think of the book "Outliers" by Malcolm Gladwell when preparing my lessons. In it, he discusses extremely successful people and the things they did to get to where they are. He argues against innate ability: the Beatles weren't incredible musicians just because they were touched by the divine, and Bill Gates wasn't an extremely successful programmer just because that's how his brain is put together. Their successes were made possible by the thousands of hours spent honing their crafts. Gladwell estimates that the number of hours Paul McCartney and John Lennon spent performing at county fairs and small German clubs before getting on TV, and the number of hours Bill Gates spent practicing computer programming on his school computer before starting to do it professionally, to be near 10,000. That's 10,000 hours of practice before becoming able to be incredible at what they do.

That's a lot of practice. Luckily, it's not as much as you might think. When I first arrived in Tokyo, I was desperate for a job. I accepted a position at Berlitz, a business-English eikaiwa, for one specific reason: they offered a part-time contract with flexible hours and bonus lessons were paid at a higher rate than if I were to be a full-time employee. I opened my schedule up completely and spent months doing 10 lesson days, grinding through lesson after lesson. When I left Berlitz, I kept my schedule full by pursuing teaching opportunities in the field I wanted to work in at the university level, pushing myself every week, spending months working **over 100 hours per week**. When I finally got my first senior high school teaching position (not as a teaching assistant but as the head teacher) I was given paid summer breaks, yet I kept working over the summer to make extra money and keep building my skills. After three years and a half years, I'd completed around 7,000 hours of teaching. As a result, I don't have classroom problems anymore. There are difficult students and difficult lessons, but I know what I need to do.

I'm not always successful, but I'm confident in the direction that I should move in. I'm able to achieve better results and become a person who can be counted upon.

If there's one thing I'd like to impart on you it's that this is not a get rich quick scheme. This is a guide to building a successful, lifelong career that you are proud of and happy with. Don't expect to be fresh off the plane, *Lonely Planet* guide in tow, and jump right into your successful teaching career. Building your skills is an extremely important step, or else even if you are given that dream opportunity you desperately desire, you won't be able to do it well, and may even end up blowing your big break. That's also why anyone reading this guide who has long been in the dredges of low-pay/high-bureaucratic eikaiwa or ALT work and not sure how to escape, your time has not been wasted. You have built a level of expertise that no degree can match, even if you may need that degree for future opportunities.

How am I qualified to give this of advice? Because I've used this sort of active career management to rise to all sorts of challenges. After finishing graduate school, I moved to San Francisco with $400 in my bank account and not a single professional contact on the west coast. I rented a room with no shower or toilet alongside the MUNI, a light rail train system that made the floorboards rumble every fifteen minutes it went by. It was late 2010 and the height of the economic recession, making finding jobs through traditional methods next to impossible. What I had was a little political experience from college internships, so I got to work building on that. I learned the lay of the diverse political landscape that is San Francisco and then found out which elected officials were running for re-election that year. I purposely chose re-election because my ultimate goal was to get into government, not work endlessly on campaigns.

Once I found my candidates, I started attending their public events, and by doing additional research I discovered which political consultancies they used. With this information and by using social networking and sending emails, I landed in the office of a political consultant, being offered minimum wage to make phone calls. A candidate was launching a new community initiative but was having trouble getting the word out. The launch would be in less than two weeks and press would be there, so we needed as big a turnout as possible.

"Make as many phone calls as it takes," they told me. I was given a voter registration list, a telephone, and a dollar store notepad. The spreadsheet included phone numbers for every resident in San Francisco county, a massive, unmanageable list. To work smarter, I used filters to pare down the spreadsheet, limiting it only to residents who were registered members of the same party as my candidate. Next, to increase the likelihood that the people I called would be politically active, I excluded anyone who had not made a political donations of at least $100 in the past two election cycles. Finally, to get rid of people who were no longer residents, I removed those who had not voted in the last election. This left me with a far better list and increased my chances of success.

Over the next ten days I made over 5,000 phone calls. This averages into a call a minute, for nine hours a day, day after day, asking strangers to come to a political event for a politician they'd never heard of. The first five hundred cold calls were terrifying. I was bothering people during meals, advocating for one candidate when they were already supporting another, injecting politics into their lives. But I kept dialing. It took 5,000 phone calls to get 113 people to show up, but a small crowd look big on television. On the day of the event, the candidate thanked me. One year later I was sitting at my desk in San Francisco City Hall, meeting with community leaders to discuss some of the biggest issues in the city.

I parlayed these lessons into coffees and cocktail when I arrived in Washington, DC. Once again, without any network or contacts, though now with my political experience in San Francisco to begin to shape my brand image, I secured a position in a Senator's office within 30 days. There are ivy league graduates, lawyers, business people, military veterans, and the children of very wealthy families, all vying for Capitol Hill positions.

Why did I get the job while they didn't?

A personal touch. I learned how Capitol Hill emails are formatted and used online. I also learned where to find physical resources to discover staff names. To do this, I had to send dozens of emails using every combination of first and last names until my request for a coffee went through. I checked my university alumni records and old newsletters to find fellow graduates who were now working in DC and started with them. I never framed these meetings as job-seeking, but rather as information seeking. A lot of people were happy to take meetings and offer their knowledge and expertise, and this experience more than any other taught me the importance of being generous with your time.

I forged relationships, made impressions, and would not finish my coffee without getting the names of at least two other people I could reach out to for more information. I held over 65 coffee meetings in those thirty days, and amassed enough Congressional business cards that you might mistake me for a lobbyist.

And the truth is, I was. I was lobbying for myself.

Using this guide to get the best jobs in Japan

I used these research and information gathering skills once again after I quit my first job in Japan. I'd been in the country for three months, located in a small, countryside town on the island of Shikoku. This wasn't the countryside we see in old samurai movies or Ghibli films: It was a desperate place, full of senior citizens, a run-down main street, and abandoned factories filled with rust, moss, and cicada carcasses. It had been a port town in the 1950s, but now had no industry other than exporting udon noodles. My job had me teaching uninterested children colors and numbers in stuffy classrooms several miles from my home, and it really wasn't my pace at all. After one particularly grueling class, caring for a room full of four year olds who were simultaneously crying, shouting, running, and wetting themselves, I decided this was not the kind of teaching I wanted to be in.

I resigned, and the next night I bought a green car ticket on the Nozomi bullet train to Shinagawa Station in Tokyo.

I spent the four hour train ride researching the Tokyo metropolitan area job market. As I went along, I was, applying for positions on my cell phone. I arrived in downtown Tokyo in the late afternoon. It was August and I was dragging a large, heavy suitcase onto and off of the Yamanote Line, sweaty and lost. I stopped by the Sakura House headquarters in Shinjuku and rented a room in Asakusa. It took me twice as long as it should have to get to where I was going after getting lost on the subway. When I arrived at the correct stop, I purchased a bento from a conbini down the street from my new place, stumbled into my new room without greeting my fellow housemates, turned the air conditioning on high, and fell asleep. **By the time I woke up I found that I had already lined up five job interviews for the next day, my first full day in Tokyo.** By the end of my first week I'd secured three offers.

Fast forward to one year later, and I was being offered a solo teaching position at one of the most prestigious senior high schools in the country. A year after that I was lecturing on political communication at a famous graduate institution in Minato Ward. A year after that I was accepting an offer to teach international affairs at a university and fielding offers at other schools. It's all possible if you put in the effort and keep moving forward. To help guide you through your journey of professional accomplishment, this book, full of Charlie and Martin's excellent advice, will help prepare you to get in the way of opportunities and begin to make your own.

How to use this book

This is a roadmap for launching & accelerating your career in Japan.

Thank you so much for picking up this guide to teaching English in Japan. You have made an important step in your teaching career in Japan by investing in yourself and your learning, and it is a step we promise you will benefit from for years to come. **Disclaimer**: Parts of this book were written and distributed through the Live Work Play Japan website. These sections only make up a small part of this book.

When we first realized we wanted to write this book, the main question we wanted to address is this:

"Can you make a decent enough wage to live comfortably **and** save for the future while working in Japan, even if you do not know Japanese?"

The answer is yes, you can! Throughout this guide we'll be dispelling myths about teaching English in Japan and giving you the tools you need to make more money, have more free time and learn valuable skills that will benefit you, not only in your time in Japan, but for the rest of your life.

Whether you are from the US, the UK, Canada or Australia, the Philippines or Timbuktu, whether you are a long term resident of Japan or are only just exploring the idea of going to Japan now, this book will serve as a road map for you to navigate your career in Japan.

As a guiding principle for starting Live Work Play Japan, Charlie and Martin see Japan as a land bursting with opportunities for both Japanese and non-Japanese alike.

There is a lot of misinformation floating around on the web that if you are a "foreigner," you can only teach English and will barely make enough to survive. There are those that will say that only people from certain western countries can be successful in Japan. We wrote this book to show you some of the career paths available and to help you on your journey to a fantastic experience living and working in Japan.

We hope you will revisit this book at different points in your career in Japan

The advice in this book is going to be valid at different points in your journey here, and we go into detail about every career stage. If you are just starting out here, some of this book will not be relevant to you yet, and if you have been here for a long time then the sections about getting to Japan will obviously be moot. Don't worry about understanding everything the first time around if you are new to this, and remember that even though our globalized world brings us closer together, living in a foreign country is still and incredibly tough and complicated thing to do. It isn't for everyone, and some people will struggle. A lot of foreigners come here to teach straight out of university, and if that is you then you are doubly brave for learning both how to be in the workforce and how to live in a foreign country at the same time.

A lot of Japanese companies know this and take advantage of new graduates' inexperience in the workplace, but there are just too many excellent opportunities in Japan to get stuck in the first company you land on here unless you actually really enjoy it.

Clearing the fog of war and showing you the options

We want to cover everything so that you can use this guide throughout your Japan experience. You'll probably start by finding a lot of jobs boards and recruiters, and we will cover some of the main ones you should know like Jobs in Japan, GaijinPot and others. We'll show you how to use these resources, craft your resume or CV with a strong narrative and give you what you need to succeed at interview.

But by itself, this guide will not be able to make a job magically land in your lap. One of the biggest issues people face in their job search, not only in Japan, is that they expect a lot for very little. Tell me if this story sounds familiar:

"I wrote my resume and put it up on all of the major job sites. I looked through the jobs and applied to 100+ positions in Tokyo and only got a few callbacks for the ones that didn't pay so well. I went to the interviews ready to answer questions about where I see myself in five years and what my weaknesses are. Now I don't know what to do or where to find other job opportunities, so I think I'll just have to stick at my ¥230,000/month eikaiwa job that sucks, but at least it pays the bills."

Unfortunately this kind of story is all too common in Japan. Nobody ever showed us how to be effective in our job search. In this book, we will show you how to get yourself in front of people who are looking for candidates just like you, and not get stuck by the gatekeepers who don't have the power to hire you. We'll explain why blasting out hundreds of resumes to every position on a jobs board will prevent you from standing out, and how to really crush it with your resume that you send to just five schools that you passionately want to work at. We'll give you scripts for contacting people in positions to help you get a job, and advice for networking with long-term expats in Japan who are connected enough to get you some of the best paying jobs you'll ever see in Japan. There's no reason to get stuck teaching somewhere that not only makes you miserable, but doesn't help you learn and grow to build a better career for your future.

Is More Money The Answer?

Live Work Play Japan isn't all about the work. There's Live and Play in there as well. We believe in finding success in all facets of your life, and that means having an amazing life experience in Japan as well. As Charlie learned, after a certain income level, more money shouldn't always be your driving force. He let himself choose a job based solely on the ¥300,000/month salary and found it to be too soul-crushing to bear. But then when he made a decision to work for a school whose message he truly believed in, he somehow wound up making more money than he had ever made in his career. Choosing your work based on lifestyle and free time can be the best choice you can make.

Charlie also invited his good friend Diego to contribute on the world of university teaching. Aside from getting several months of paid vacation, it is not unheard of for lecturers to rake in more than ¥500,000 a month as a starting salary. Martin worked as a bilingual real estate broker in Tokyo, and while there, he saw the tax returns of many expats. Among them, university teachers had some of the highest demonstrable incomes of all the expats he saw. Not only do you pull in the big bucks teaching at university, but you can easily get two or three months of paid vacation as well as generous health, pension and travel benefits. We'll go through that more later in the book.

Whatever you do learn from this book, we will be putting all of the resources, links and bonus extra content on our site at liveworkplayjapan.com/teach-english.

But I'm Not A Native English Speaker...

A quick word to our readers from countries like India, the Philippines and Romania. First off, thanks for picking up this book. We appreciate that you are reading and we hope you give us plenty of feedback. Many of you may be wondering:

"If I am not a native English speaker, do I even have a chance of getting a good job in Japan?"

Let's just talk about English teaching as an example for now. The answer is yes, you can definitely get an ESL (English as a Second Language) job paying ¥280,000 and above. You can even teach at a university like Charlie's long time friend Vey-Yin from Singapore.

In the beginning, and especially for young people, it can be hard to get your first legs in Japan when you are not a native speaker. It is hard enough for an Australian or Canadian to get a job teaching English in Japan with the kind of salary we are talking about getting in this book. It is even harder for those of you who are not considered natives, but it is possible if you have the skills and know how to present yourself. This book will help to teach you how to do that.

Do not be dismayed by the difficult start, but make the decision to bring change to your life. Follow the guidelines we set in this book closely and carefully read later where we talk about success stories from other non-native English speakers like yourself. We have worked with and for non-native English speakers in Japan. It is only impossible if you believe it is impossible.

If you are not a native speaker of English, I will say that any accreditation and recommendation you get will be a big help to you. Of course, this goes the same for our friends from the US, Canada and Britain, but doubly so for non-natives where forms of proof can help to bring your profile up and to exceed the natural qualifications that native English speakers are privileged to have. For you, we highly recommend you consider a TEFL course of some kind and that you continually seek out education in the field of teaching. Checking sites like the **Oxford University Press** for seminars is a great way not only to network in Japan, but to get accredited further in the teaching field.

Whatever path you take, this book will help you to find better opportunities in Japan.

If you want to move into other industries

This is exactly what both Charlie and Martin have been doing for more than a year now, and while Charlie loves teaching and still has his hand in that industry, Martin has moved out of teaching using his Japanese skills. We will talk more about Japanese and the methods and strategies to learn it. Japanese language ability isn't necessary to apply a lot of what is in this book, but it is absolutely unquestionable that it can help you grow your career whether you are still teaching English or if you want to move into a Japanese company, or even starting your own company or school where you will need to work closely with Japanese people (big money can be made here).

Explore your options with us in this book and be open to the change that we are trying to make. None of this matters if it isn't applied, just like reading a book about how to ride bicycles won't help you to start pedaling. Be bold and apply the strategies to find your success.

一緒に頑張りましょう

Isshou ni gambarimashou

Why Japan?

If you are reading this you probably already know the answer to this question.

You don't just want to live anywhere in Asia - it has always been Japan for you.

You have dreamed of living in Japan, experiencing the culture and learning the Japanese language since you were little.

Maybe you practiced eating every grain in a bowl of rice with chopsticks when you were a kid. Or maybe you tried watching anime without subtitles and got excited every time you heard a word or sentence you understood. Maybe you met some Japanese people in your hometown or at your university, and they made a real impact on you. You might be a big fan of tradition and have fallen head-over-heels in love with the magical and unique way that Japan blends and blurs the lines between their traditional roots and their modern technological splendour. Whatever your reasons may be, nothing else will do. Korea looks like fun and it's cheaper to live, Vietnam has a great expat community and Thailand has amazing food, but Japan is where you want to be.

In addition to your passion for this country, there are many other compelling reasons to choose Japan as a place to teach English over other Asian countries.

Japan has one of the highest salary rates for English teachers.

Average monthly wages for English teachers in Asia

S. Korea -$2100/m

China -$1450/m

Japan -$3000/m

Saudi Arabia -$4000/m

Thailand -$1000/m

Vietnam -$1500/m

Information sourced at: http://www.internationalteflacademy.com/country-chart-world-index-english-teaching-jobs

Salaries in Japan are quite high on a global scale, but cost of living can be high particularly in popular destinations like Tokyo, Yokohama and Osaka. Yet those with high paying jobs are still able to take home 10-20% or more in savings, or even more if you live a minimalist lifestyle. That is why it is crucial to be placed well in a high paying job.

Japanese culture is amazing.

I've never been to a country with such varied culture depending on the region. Fukuoka has a very different feel to Tokyo. Hokkaido is like a completely different country. Okinawa is like a beautiful tropical paradise, more comparable to Hawaii than mainland Japan.

There is so much to explore here, and because of the Shinkansen bullet trains and great public transport system it is easy to see so many different places while living here. Whether you are interested in Japanese Tea Ceremony, learning Kendo (swordfighting) or Kyuudo (archery), there are a million and one things to do here that you can only experience in Japan.

Japan has one of the most varied and internationally prized cuisines in the world.

After he moved to Japan Charlie lost almost 10kg (20 pounds) and kept it off. 和風 Wafuu; Japanese food - is not only incredibly varied and delicious, but also much healthier than most western foods. It is generally served in smaller portions that, once you get used to it, will be a welcome relief from overeating.

There are some truly unique Japanese foods that you absolutely must try, whether you live here or you are just travelling.

The food is and always has been Martin's absolute favorite thing about Japan. He has been all over Asia and in other countries around the world and no one seems to get Japanese food right.

Japanese are in love with the idea of 四季 *shiki* - the four seasons, so if you go to a Japanese grocery store you will notice that there are new foods in season almost every single month. The entire food culture is in harmony with nature.

You cannot get the same experience abroad.

Seriously, *real* Japanese food is unique to Japan.

Yaki-niku, Shabu-shabu, sushi, sashimi, okonomiyaki, 祭り *matsuri* street food dishes, ramen in thousands of varieties, oden, udon, soba... The list goes on. You will never know the seasonal variety, serving style and ambiance that goes with them until you come to Japan.

A short holiday will only leave you just wanting more, so

without further adieu let's look at the kind of people this book aims to help.

Who is this guide for?

Japan is not like the West, so it makes sense that there would be a learning curve to figuring out the job market here. The problem for so many people wanting to come to Japan is that the learning curve is so steep that it can seem impossible to start moving up.

Maybe you are outside Japan, looking in and worrying about speaking Japanese or how to find jobs that will help you pay your student loans. Perhaps you've been here a while and you're sick of your low-paying or unrewarding job. After receiving so many emails from people who feel stuck in their entry-level English teaching jobs, we wrote this guide to help foreigners in Japan to get their talents recognised.

This guide will be useful to anyone looking to find a better job teaching English in Japan, but let's break down the path of a few different kinds of people who come to Japan. If you've been here for a little while you know someone just like all of the people below, or you might be one of them. Let's start with Joe:

Joe

Joe doesn't live in Japan. He grew up in Pennsylvania and just finished his degree. He went to a seminar about the JET program in his final year of college and thought it sounded interesting, but he can't speak any Japanese and didn't want to take the risk of going to a foreign country straight out of college without getting some real experience in the workplace first. He has a job in the head office of a major retailer, but he hates it and imagines himself flying over to Japan, exploring temples and climbing Mt.Fuji in the summer. He actually went to Japan on a holiday and it was everything he dreamed it would be and more. He wants to go and live there but he has no idea how to do it.

"How do I get a job in Japan? How do I get the visa? Can I be an English teacher even though my degree is in business management?"

These are all questions that Joe asks himself as he continues to work in his boring office job. While all of his friends and co-workers talk about moving up the corporate ladder or living for the weekend, Joe wants to get away from his desk and have an adventure!

Khalinda

Khalinda is originally from Punjab, but grew up in Australia speaking English. Now she lives in Hiroshima prefecture in Japan, in a small town outside of the main city. She came to live here two years ago and started working for an eikaiwa (English conversation school) where she works evenings and weekends teaching kids of all ages. She loves Japan, the food and the culture, and has a few Japanese friends that she hangs out with at the local darts bar. However, her town is very rural, and her apartment feels like it is in the middle of nowhere, a 20-minute walk from the station.

Khalinda's job is also very unrewarding, and she really wants to have an impact in the kind of teaching she is doing. She just doesn't know how to get out of her current job and find something that allows her to live in the city, and pays her enough money to put some into savings while also paying off her student loans. She has had some trouble getting interviews and she wonders if it is because she looks Indian, as many Japanese people she meets assume that she doesn't speak English, which is ridiculous because English is one of India's national languages.

So she continues to work for her school, and feels more and more like giving up and just going home. She just doesn't want to go out like that. Her little sister who didn't go to college is already making more money than her back home working in an office in Sydney, so her innate competitive nature makes her feel like she should be doing better.

A lot of Khalinda's friends who expatriated to Japan tell her that it's impossible to get paid more as an English teacher unless she goes back to university and gets her Master's in TEFL or she could learn to speak Japanese and becomes a "salary-woman". She doesn't want to work in an office, nor go back to school as she doesn't have the two years or the savings to get such an expensive qualification.

Khalinda has met a few people who are making great money in International schools and private schools in Osaka and Tokyo, and she wonders if she could make that kind of money if she just moved to the city and tried.

George

George is from Manchester in the UK, and he came to Japan after a few years in the private sector following university. He started off in an eikaiwa much like Khalinda, but he sought out other options almost immediately when he realized that he could make more money and enjoy his life more in the city. In less than six months he was living in a one room apartment in Yokohama, commuting to Tokyo to work in a big public school.

George picked up a TEFL qualification online after his first year in Japan and used that on his resume to get better and better school positions. He makes friends with a lot of people in Tokyo, and finally makes the move into Tokyo city proper to make more connections and avoid the long commutes from "the Yokes" as he and his friends had fondly come to call Yokohama.

George switched full-time jobs a few times but finally realized after three years in Japan that he could make much more money using his network and by mixing and matching part-time jobs. Through friends and connections he got jobs that others say only go to people with Master's degrees or a

PhD, but now that he has been in Japan for five years he knows that the most important thing is knowing people and having a proven and supported record of great results.

He teaches in several schools landing a few highly sought after gigs at a university connected high schools. On Monday and Wednesday he teaches at one, and then Tuesday and Friday he teaches at the other, and he has a few seasonal jobs teaching returnees or students travelling abroad. He makes an average of ¥490,000 a month, has six weeks vacation in summer and a month for Christmas fully paid, plus all national holidays and a nice bonus for completing and renewing his contract.

George loves his job, and has paid off most of his student loans and is enjoying his time in Japan. With his experience, the qualifications and the accolades he has achieved, he knows that if he can find other jobs should he need to, and if he ever left Japan he could easily find interesting and rewarding work back home.

Which one are you?

Whether you are in a similar situation to Joe, Khalinda or someone else, we can learn to replicate what George has done. **He has a firm grasp of his market value.** He understands how to find opportunities in Japan's English teaching job market because he can see when and where he can position himself. George doesn't have to know everything about Japan, he just needs to know how to win at the game. He learned the rules that apply to teachers in Japan, as well as which ones can be bent, and which can be broken.

This book seeks to arm you with the knowledge of the tools that help you build your career

That is what we want to teach with this book. We want to show you a roadmap for success English teaching in Japan and beyond. With the knowledge you gain from reading this, you will be in a much better position to be more like George, and live the kind of life that works for you in Japan. And all this doesn't mean that you need to teach English forever, and should you ever want to make the transition back to your home country (or anywhere else for that matter), what you learn here will be valuable and applicable for the rest of your life.

Remember: If you listen to the naysayers who tell you that there is no way for you to succeed here, then you may end up bitter and resentful like they are. Martin and Charlie have experienced all of this first hand and can tell you that the right psychological thinking is crucial to your ability to find success in Japan.

The good news is that by picking up this book you have already taken a step towards mastering the psychology of success. If you continue to believe that you can have the kind of life you want in Japan, and apply the strategies and techniques we will teach you, you'll start to see results.

You need to actually apply all of this in the real world. Even if you read this book cover to cover, it isn't enough to get the kind of job you want here in Japan. You need to go out and use it. We will root for your success.

Don't be a "Give-up Gaijin"

Let's imagine an English teacher named Jeff. Jeff arrived in Japan in his 20s and accepted the first teaching job he was offered, maybe at an eikaiwa or as an ALT. The pay wasn't great but the hours were good and he had enough money to pick up a few cans of Chu-Hai every week. He met a nice girl who was satisfied with dates at Saizeriya or an occasional dalliance at a low-cost love hotel in Ikebukuro. Jeff is happy and comfortable, and before he knows it five years have gone by. He starts to think about what skills he has developed that can transfer over to a career back in his home country. His relationship has grown more serious and now he and his girlfriend are discussing marriage. His salary has increased by about ¥200 an hour, enough to afford him an occasional night at the movies and a new phone every two years.

Fast forward another five years and now Jeff is in his mid thirties. He has a wife and two kids to support and has to commute three hours a day so that he can afford an apartment big enough for his family. His salary has remained relatively unchanged and he lives paycheck-to-paycheck. He can't afford to get sick as one missed day would reduce his pay for the month and he has taught the same, boring materials more times that he can count. He still cannot find a way to transfer his skills over into a new career and he can't take risks at this point anyway - his family is his top priority. Unless he takes action to change his situation, this will be the way he lives until he retires at 65 and starts collecting his ¥70,000 per month government pension.

Over time, Jeff has become bitter about his prospects in Japan. He feels stuck. It is too late for him to go home and start over now. Yet, he doesn't know where to go, and he has found himself hitting a ceiling in Japan. Jeff has given up on finding a life he loves in Japan and, to the outside observer, seems like he wants to drag down everyone else with him.

It's easy to get comfortable, especially in a country like Japan. Weekend ski trips and holidays eating roasted pork and sweet plums, walking along ancient temples with your partner can make anyone feel like they're living a rich life. They are, but do not confuse complacency with security. The hard truth is that there is a very limited future available if you remain at an eikaiwa or as an ALT for very long, and the realities of family, old age, illness, or ambition will push the obscured limits of your lifestyle. Working these jobs is a fine way to build teaching experience, to start off your career in Japan, but staying in them long term will lead to a difficult life with many hardships and impossible decisions.

Hard decisions lead to an easy life; easy decisions lead to a hard life. Make the hard decisions now.

Money is not the most important thing in life, but it is high on the list. Affording a comfortable home, sending your kids to a good school, caring for your parents in their old age, getting a car, going on vacation, or even the luxury of someday not working, all depend on what you can do now to set yourself up for the kind of life you desire.

When you meet Jeff, take his advice with a grain of salt. Know that you can choose to do better and avoid his mistakes using the thoughtful and longer-term approach that we are talking about in this book.

Getting to Japan

Landing a Job from outside Japan

The first step for many people will be to get a job from outside Japan. This is how Charlie did it and it can be one of the fastest ways to get a job, but it is highly unlikely to get you the best paying or most fun kind of work. But that's no problem! **Once you are in Japan you can find other jobs much more easily.**

Being in Japan is the best way to get jobs here, as a lot of schools and companies will not want to pay extra to sponsor a visa and help move you to Japan and get you set up. But there are some that will, and those are the schools we will focus on for now. There are a few big companies but we'll talk about the ones that have a low barrier to entry so you can get yourself to Japan. While we always recommend finishing your contract so your resume looks good, it's totally up to you. Legally you just need to give a month of notice at least to get out of your contract, which is covered in the Civil Code of Japan. Check the resources for this book at **liveworkplayjapan.com/teach-english** for links to our working rights article with legal sources and evidence for this.

If the job is okay and you like it, then you can stick around, but as we said being in Japan and having that visa is key. We'll talk about this later but your visa belongs to you and not your company; they can't take it away from you no matter what, so once you have it you can look for other jobs if you want to.

Main Requirement - Having a Bachelor's Degree

For better or for worse, the overwhelming majority of schools require you to have a Bachelor's degree if you want to apply for a job with them. If you don't have one you're looking at an uphill battle, but by no means is it impossible. It is simply harder to get a foreign visa sponsored without a bachelor's degree. With determination and persistence on your side, you can land well paying jobs in Japan without one, but you will have to use all the tools at your disposal to get in front of more qualified candidates. It is possible, and Charlie's good friend Mike is working at a prestigious school in Tachikawa city after coming here on a working holiday visa (and a job connection through a friend), then getting married and obtaining a spousal visa within the first year of coming to Japan. We'll talk more about using your network, your best asset for getting jobs in Japan, later on in the book.

The reason for the general requirement of a bachelor's degree is mostly due to the visa applications procedure, but the hope is also that it would guarantee a certain level of skill from applicants. I've seen a lot of teachers with Bachelor's degrees do a terrible job, but that's the bar the Japanese government has set. If you meet the requirements of speaking English at a native or near native level and have a degree, congratulations! You're ready to teach English! No you're not, but for the sake of coming to Japan and doing it you have approval.

Overseas Placements

JET Program - highly sought after and competitive

The Japan Exchange & Teaching Programme is run by the **MEXT** (The Ministry of Education, Culture, Sports, Science and Technology in Japan, don't ask why it isn't the

MECSST). If you are thinking of moving to Japan or live here, chances are you've already heard of the JET program. It's a government run organisation that brings foreigners from around the world to Japan to teach English in public schools. Their organisation is large and they have a very selective interview process that takes almost a year.

The JET program pays better than your standard job coming to Japan. General starting salary is ¥300,000 per month with generous allowances for your apartment and possibly a car if you live in a rural community, but there are also a lot of expectations. Teachers usually live in the countryside and there are fewer opportunities for advancement unless you speak fluent Japanese, a difficult task even when you live here. Your visa is also tied to your employment in the JET program, so if you plan to leave the program you'll have to find another sponsor to renew your visa within 90 days or you'll have to leave Japan.

Leaving the JET program is harder than leaving other jobs as they do not take kindly to people leaving mid-contract. I've only heard of one case where somebody left midway through their contract and that was because there was a mix-up with their school and there was nothing for them to do (they were doing office tasks all day). For those reasons we think that finding a job on your own rather than going through the JET program is the fastest way to set yourself up for success in Japan. If you have the time to spare or you can apply in your last year of university, and then apply for the JET program.

A little disclaimer: Neither Charlie nor Martin ever worked for the JET Program. Martin did apply for the CIR (Coordinator for International Relations) job with the JET Program but ultimately never got to the interview despite having the JLPT (Japanese Language Proficiency Test) level 2 at the time. It is hard to get an interview with JET no matter if you speak Japanese or not, but the rewards can be amazing as you may read online. JETs will be in nearly every community in Japan, and you get an added benefit of joining in a long tradition of JETs from all over the globe.

At the time of writing you can only remain as a JET for five years, so it cannot be a long term plan for building a career in Japan. In this book we are focussing on work outside of JET, so if you want more information check the JET website.

The largest English teaching employers in Japan

> **Aeon**

Aeon is massive in Japan, and most well known for their huge malls that are ubiquitous all over the country. They have a long history of English teaching in Japan and you can see their advertisements plastered up in the trains here all year long. They mostly cater to adult and business English learners, but they also have Aeon Kids, where young learners can learn English too. They hire throughout the year and will sponsor a visa.

Go to their website at aeonet.com

> **ECC**

In the same line as Aeon, ECC offers classes for both adults and kids and recruits throughout the year. As with many eikaiwa (English conversation schools), most of the lessons will be in the evenings and on weekends.

Their website is at eccteachinjapan.com

➢ Interac

Interac is pretty well known in Japan and has business English schools as well as being one of the top dispatch companies that send ALTs (Assistant Language Teachers) to Elementary, Junior High and High schools in Japan.

Martin's first ALT experience was with this company. Interac serves almost like a broker for English teachers. Chiefly among the services they render is to provide ALTs to school boards. They also provide basic training for freshmen teachers as well as on-going training for contract teachers.

"At first it felt like a pain going to the monthly Interac training sessions. But it wasn't without the perk of being able to skip some of your afternoon classes, and once I got to know more ALTs in the area it got to be a lot of more fun. It was a time when all the local ALTs would get together with our advisor trainers and share new techniques, games and methods that were working for us.

They have so many connections now, some teachers even teach directly to salary-men at their large companies. It's a big growing company, a lot of opportunities to rise in the ranks well beyond just teaching English. Corporate is within reach too if you pick up Japanese. Interac. Overall, not a bad place to work at all."

Their website is at interacnetwork.com

➢ Berlitz

Berlitz is one of the biggest global language learning companies, with schools all throughout Japan. They focus on adult and business English but they also have kids classes. They have a very good reputation and have a pretty reasonable starting salary rate, but it is also quite competitive.

Their site is at teach.berlitz.co.jp

More examples of employers that hire from overseas

> **Peppy Kid's Club**

I (Charlie) started off my teaching career in Japan at Peppy Kid's Club, and to their credit the training was fantastic. They had a full two weeks of intensive training, and while I still didn't feel ready to walk into a classroom after that, it was a lot more than any other school I've taught at since.

Peppy doesn't do big advertising and relies heavily on their sales team, but they have thousands of classrooms across Japan and their own curriculum. If you work at Peppy you'll get a lot of experience of working with kids, plus a lot of time to build up your teaching skills. Honestly when I applied for an international pre-school my demo made an incredible impression with the Encho-sensei (pre-school principal), simply because I had practiced so many of them during my time at Peppy.

It is a very good place to start in Japan, and while they do have some bureaucratic nonsense to put up with, I have never heard of a teacher being given a hard time for leaving early (which is what I did). They were professional and I could move out of the company apartment with plenty of time to find my own space.

They accept applications year round, with their site at ittti.com/pkc/

> **Altia**

Altia is one of the biggest dispatch companies for ALTs in Japan. They send teachers to Elementary, Junior High and High schools to assist in English language instruction. Their pay is generally a little on the low side (¥240,000 a month) but they hire from overseas and will help get you started in Japan.

Their site is at recruiting.altmoot.com

• **Gaba & Nova**

Both of these schools are owned by Jibun Mirai Associe after both were bought out after their embarrassing financial troubles in the past. Being a teacher at Nova was particularly rough at that time. After failing to pay over 6000 teachers for several months, they filed for bankruptcy in 2010. Now both companies still own and operate several hundred schools in Japan and internationally, and their brand names still carry a lot of weight for Japanese people.

Gaba has their site at gabateachinginjapan.com and Nova is at nova.co.jp. Both have similar applications processes with links on those two pages. I'll let you make up your own minds about them. I've met a few teachers in both companies and they don't seem to be having any problems now. Do your own research and read what people who have worked for them recently have to say.

Finding a job from outside Japan couldn't be easier in this day and age. Use the companies above or go on JobsinJapan.com or GaijinPot and look for companies that say they will hire from overseas. Once you get here, the task of finding your real job begins. Check the next page for the key features of working for JET or at private companies:

JET	Both	Private Companies
Employed by Japanese Government	Usually offers assistance to apply for work visa	Employed by private and publicly traded companies
Living assistance provided	Can use applications for apartment guarantor	Living assistance rarely provided
Low chance of employer not paying your salary	Co-payment for health insurance and pension	Slightly higher chance of employer defaulting on salary payments
Above average starting salary		Median starting salary, higher potential salary
Limited contract renewals		Unlimited contract renewals, often with bonuses or pay rises if you negotiate
Location preferences not considered a priority		You can change jobs easily to find one in the city you'd like to live
Only public school teaching		Public and private school teaching
Represent your country in an official capacity in Japan		You represent yourself

Job Searching from Inside Japan

Looking for a job once you are here is **by far** the best way to get a job in Japan. Believe it or not, most companies in Japan don't want to spend thousands of dollars sponsoring a visa for an unproven and untested teacher. Go figure... Even if you already have a company and moved to Japan with your visa sorted, you don't have to stick around with the first company you signed with, especially if you aren't making the kind of compensation that you could make at another job.

If you're already here and you've been teaching for a year or more, you have a million and one more opportunities that you had when you were applying from overseas and didn't have your visa. One of our friends came to Japan with a three year visa in hand, and quit his company in the first six months. The school was upset but he ended up getting a much better teaching position in Tokyo, living in the city he dreamed of living in and getting paid more than he could have ever gotten sticking with the company that brought him to Japan.

Moving up the ladder as an English teacher within a company can be very hard and doesn't always yield the kind of salary increase that would make the extra time worth it. I still have friends working for the same company as they were in when they arrived in Japan. After five years or more, they might still be in the same position with only cost of living increases for the time they have been there. For some it is even worse, they got promoted to a management position where they no longer teach but work in an office as a

サラリーマン (salaryman - the Japanese word for office worker). The salary takes a little step up, maybe a 10% increase over the English teaching rate, but the hours leap up to 40 or 50 hours per week with the added responsibilities and (unpaid) overtime work.

This is why looking for jobs from within Japan is the best way to get a better salary and learn more while you are here. Sticking it out with your company and moving up the corporate ladder will take years and is unlikely to give you the kind of salary you can make using the strategies we'll talk about later.

Your new job is called "get a great job" and yes, you have to put in the hours. What are you doing waking up at 2pm on your off days, watching TV and then updating LinkedIn and sending out a few emails? Do you think that is enough to get yourself a job here? Set hours for yourself and an agenda. The system doesn't have to be too complicated. If you just worked this like a job a little bit of the time, you will have more job offers than you know what to with within a month or two.

Read more books about the job climate

Aside from obviously the book you are reading now, you'll need to be well read and understand the market here. Pick an industry like English teaching (or whatever else you want to move into) and learn who are the top, middle and stand-out players. Learn where they are located. Read reviews about them and reach out to them. Do loads of research on companies that are looking for applicants. Read more books about the job climate.

For your first jobs in Japan as an inexperienced teacher, jobs boards are going to be your go-to. Look up what kinds of jobs there are and start applying. Set quotas. You are marketing yourself. Set targets at which to reward yourself, like getting an ice cream when you apply to ten companies per day. If I don't reach my target then you have to apply to twenty companies the next day. This doesn't mean you blast out your resume to a bunch of companies and call it a day. You have to tailor your application to each one, fix up your resume and alter your cover letters. We will talk about building your resume later on.

Don't give yourself even a chance to use the excuse that you are too busy at work. If you work between 7am and 4pm as a kindergarten teacher, there are plenty of schools and companies open until 5, 7 even 10pm or they will accommodate you if they like you and if you reach out to them using the strategies we talk about later in this book. It's even easier if you are working evenings. Wake up early and you'll have the mornings to go to schools or companies and hand in your resume. Plenty of international schools and kindergartens open on Saturdays for club activities too.

The key is to plan what you will do with your time. Don't let hours of inactive time build up in your day until you've achieved your goal. Remember that you don't have to settle but you do have to hustle. The way to get those job offers, even if you don't have a working visa yet, is to meet people who can connect you to companies looking for your skills.

Follow companies on social and ask for help when you need it. You want to connect with and start sending connect requests to potential employers or people who could get you in contact with employers. I would do this on LinkedIn, Facebook and Twitter. Set a quota for fifteen requests a day until you get a sizeable network. LinkedIn and Facebook groups are great places to find relevant people to connect with. Engage people there, ask questions on Facebook groups and forums. The reddit group **r/teachinginjapan** is run by some great people and they are much more receptive and less toxic than some of the old Japan forums where "give-up gaijin" go to vent. Tokyo Expat Network on Facebook is also a very helpful group of people who will point you in the right direction.

Check out Meetup.com

Find fun groups and relevant groups to go to. Don't just limit yourself to the Japanese-English language exchanges. Do fun things like rock climbing or hiking. You'll not only meet a lot of cool Japanese locals, you'll meet people that will fill in the gaps. They will teach you things but also introduce you to jobs or people that they know that you could teach. Charlie got a great job connection from his yoga instructor, and just about anyone can be a connection worth having, especially if they have been in Japan for a long time and can teach you a thing or two.

Present yourself

Dress up

Whatever that means for you, just do your best. If you are a man, I suggest a suit for professional occasions with a tie (except in summer where you will suffocate in one). On off-days dress as well as you can when out in case you meet someone who can connect you. It gives the impression that you are already doing something important so people want to be around you. For the ladies, I am really not qualified to tell you how to dress as I figure there are millions of magazines already telling you how to do this. I suggest giving the air of a casual professional. I won't go into detail there. Just dress the best you know how to for the occasion. Tons of people know how to dress well, but few actually do. Just doing obvious stuff like this sets you apart.

Go out and meet people at events

Meetup.com is a great start. There are event sites too like doorkeeper, and with Facebook events (there is now a local search function that is really useful) there isn't really an excuse not to put yourself out there and meet people. Just look up "International Party" + your city in Japan. Of course, most are in Tokyo but there are more these days in Kansai and other regions. The parties are just parties but if you can find events that are in your industry or that are professional leadership talks or business events, these are better for finding people that can help you in your professional journey. Toastmasters even has an all English meetup, for example. I went to the Japanese language one and met CEOs from all sorts of industries.

Get the Line App

This is a must-have app for networking in Japan. Possibly even more important than Facebook, the Line app is like a Whatsapp, Facebook and Twitter all rolled in one in Japan. I haven't exchanged an actual phone number with Japanese people in years. We just use Line since it also has text and phone functionality. Just trust us and get this app, everybody in Japan has it and uses it.

Bring your 名刺

Meishi are "Business cards." Place your basic contact info especially your email and LINE ID here. If you teach a foreign language or offer a freelance service like web design, you can put your rates on on the back or the process of how to obtain your services. This card must be in Japanese and English minimum.

Show interest in other people

This is truly a rarity today, and taking the time to work on your interpersonal skills and practice listening can be the difference between never seeing an interesting business contact again and getting a warm lead on a potential job. I mean genuinely listening to and caring about the person that is talking to you. If you can actually show interest in other people, you will have no shortage of friends.

More friends means bigger network. Bigger network means your chances to offer value to that network will increase.

What is a job anyway? Just a position where you offer value to your network in exchange for compensation. Ask people about what they do, where they want to go in life and see if you might be able to help them in some way. You could teach them French, help them with a project, or just be a friend willing to listen.

Networking in Japan **in person** is an essential part of your job search. People want to put a face to a name and if all you are doing is filling out a resume form and sending it out to lots of companies, you will be as faceless as a blank piece of paper.

Remember your mission everywhere you go

Let everyone you meet know that you are here to offer your services in your industry and that is your purpose in Japan.

It's the number one question foreigners get in Japan, so you won't need to artificially insert this answer into most conversations anyway. Let them know why you're here. If you are a language teacher or aspire to be one, this can be really effective for finding connections to jobs or getting private lesson clients where your rates can be much higher than what you might make at your eikaiwa job.

Meeting your Tanaka-san (Job connection)

This is not a popularity contest, but don't forget that you are on a mission. You are not just around to be around Japan if you come here looking for a job. Your mission does not rest on Saturday. Even if you already have a job offer on the table, maybe you are seeking something better.

You might just run into Tanaka-san who is looking for a new English teacher to lead his English teaching club, or help his international sales team practice their English. Charlie teaches some execs a number of times a month and they pay him ¥10,000 each time to just talk with them in English and challenge their business discussions thoughtfully. Charlie actually does more work than this preparing some content to discuss, but the point is, you never know when you will meet your Tanaka-san.

Don't limit yourself if you want to hustle to get your own students. If you can teach something else too, mix it in. I know plenty of Japanese who pay a decent amount an hour to take salsa lessons from gaikokujin in English. ¿Habla Castellano? Add in bonus Spanish lessons. Or how about cooking? Charlie has been teaching his artisan bakery class, named **Charlie's Bread**, since February 2017. Whatever you have in your pocket, there is a way to use it in Japan.

Using Japanese

Things get a lot easier in this country if you can speak Japanese. I can't understate that. Being able to at least communicate in some way in Japanese will be a massive boon to your job search. While a Japanese school is highly unlikely to tell an English teacher that they must speak Japanese, the reality is that you will often be working with other Japanese people. Even if they speak English, being able to converse with them in their native tongue will help your relationship to work much better. We'll talk more about Japanese later on in the book, and you can get our favourite resources for learning Japanese at liveworkplayjapan.com/teach-english.

Of course if you don't know Japanese yet that is okay. Nobody is expecting you to become fluent overnight, but putting in the effort to learn is hands down one of the best ways to set yourself apart from the English teachers who are treating their time in Japan like a holiday from real life.

Kinds of English teaching jobs in Japan and what you need to get them.

The majority of foreigners go through their standard job searches and full-time salaries in Japan without ever knowing that other opportunities exist. They might never even know what basic kinds of jobs there are or what institutions hire English speaking foreigners. I can guarantee that if you've been in Japan a few years, you know some people making a killing as an English teacher in Japan.

Knowing the fundamental basics and types of English teaching jobs should be a bare minimum for you to have any chance at getting the jobs that are higher up on the hierarchy of English teaching positions. Often the best opportunities to advance are right below your nose.

Eikaiwa (英会話)

Teach your native language at an eikaiwa. The most well known examples are AEON and ECC, but there are tons of others. Eikaiwa 英会話 literally means English conversation, but don't be discouraged if you aren't a native English speaker as you can teach Chinese, French, Spanish or German as well.

You usually sit in a small classroom with the student(s) and either just have a conversation or go over materials with them. Dress is usually formal as your students are often business men and women, but will be more casual if teaching kids.

Pros:

- Often has a flexible (read: irregular) schedule.
- Low barrier to entry.
- Applications accepted all year round.

Cons:

- High turnover, companies won't hesitate to get rid of you if you give them cause.
- Lower or just average pay.
- Two-day weekends are rare (usually one day in the week and one at the weekend).
- May have cramped teaching areas.
- Formal dress usually required, and little room for creativity with company materials.

Qualifications needed:

None other than native level English (some require a degree, but this is mostly for Visa purposes). You don't need a TEFL qualification or any teaching experience to get an eikaiwa job, but of course it helps, *especially if you are a non-native speaker of English*. It will help you to do a great job once you get there and put your teaching process into words, which can lead to recommendation letters and possible promotions if you want to move up the corporate ladder in this kind of company.

Juku (塾)

Similarly, there are after school programs/schools called Juku (often referred to as cram school). A good example is Kumon, and although the environments are very similar to eikaiwa there is a key difference. You are usually in a small room prepping students for English tests like Eiken, TOEFL and TOEIC.

In Juku often the kids are already a bit worn out from school and after school sports before coming. A big part of your job isn't to just prep them for some test, but to keep them engaged. If you genuinely care, they will respond well.

Pros:

- Flexible schedule.
- Low barrier to entry.
- Applications accepted all year round.
- Easy to enter into once on the ground in Japan.
- Fits well as a part-time job.

Cons:

- Lower or just average pay.
- Two-day weekends are rare.
- Students come to you tired from school.

- Little room for creativity when using company materials.

Qualifications needed:

Similarly to eikaiwa jobs, you don't need anything other than native level English with a degree to get the visa. You don't need a TEFL qualification or any teaching experience, but for juku it is likely to help you in a big way to get the job. Qualifications play well in this more academic environment where you are preparing students for tests. You will feel more prepared and have more understanding of what students need to know to succeed in the tests, and will get better results from your students.

ALT (Assistant Language Teacher)

Teach your native language in Elementary through to High School classrooms as an assistant to the home room JT (Japanese Teacher). Many can get away without much preparation work as the JT may do it for you, but don't expect that to be the norm. Usually they want you to make activity worksheets, but responsibilities and chances to build your reputation as a great teacher are limitless.

It's not unheard of to hear of ALTs running after-school English clubs. If you played basketball in college in the States, the school will be positively excited to get you coaching the basketball squad. In many Japanese schools, the coach of a team might not even play that sport. They might just be supervising, and in Charlie's junior high job in Nagoya, the basketball coach didn't know how to shoot a ball or do a layup. This might just seem like an extra responsibility, but you never know where it could lead.

Pay varies greatly here depending on the company that places you. JETs are often ALTs and are compensated well. If you can't get into the JET program, get close with the Japanese school board while working for a dispatch company and you can make as much or more than JET ALTs by taking out the middle-man dispatch company.

Another way to earn more is to work for private schools. Japan has many and also there are private schools run by universities that pay teachers well. Start looking to apply by December and keep your ear to the ground from January to March for jobs starting in April.

Pros:

- Consistent daily schedule (8:30- 4:30) 5 days a week only.
- Almost always English teachers have holidays off.
- Not nearly as much prep work as a normal teacher.
- Feeling a sense of community and often involved in local festivals and other festivities.
- JTs often don't speak English well so you can learn and practice your Japanese.

Cons:

- Mid-level barrier to entry.
- Little to no control of curriculum.
- Not for you if you don't like kids.
- JTs rarely speak great English so you will likely need to have some Japanese ability.

Qualifications needed:

A degree is a bare minimum, but otherwise many teachers

get hired to ALT positions without any teaching qualifications or experience. For private schools that pay well, a minimum of a 120-Hour TEFL course would be a recommendation, plus a year or more of teaching to a similar age group. A lot of the skills you learn in your TEFL course will help you in these public school jobs. Lesson planning, grammar studies, and teaching for tests all become very important in junior high and high school. Many jobs like this also recommend or prefer TEFL holders for obvious reasons (more prepared to teach at this level).

JET stands for Japanese Exchange and Teaching. Most positions are for teachers as the name would suggest, which in almost all cases means an ALT.

There are now positions for sports coordinators to work with schools and the CIR (Coordinator for International Relations), a highly competitive position for those with high-level Japanese skills.

JETs are usually well compensated, a good 50-100,000¥ more per month in than the average eikaiwa or ALT teacher. JETs are usually placed in areas where few foreign teachers tend to go so if you get a JET position, welcome to the sticks!

Pros:

- High pay (first year teachers earn 280,000¥,

increases by 20,000￥ per month each year)

- Some of the same pros as the ALTs above.
- Get paid most of your pension contributions after your JET stay is over.

Cons:

- 5 year contract limit (can be a harsh drop in salary to the next job if you stay in Japan).
- Super high barrier to entry (applications start almost one year out).
- Highly competitive.
- Rural, middle-of-nowhere placements are the norm, not the exception.

Qualifications needed:

Unlike eikaiwa and similarly to other ALT positions, a university degree is a must for these positions. They are run under the watchful eye of the Japanese government, so there's no getting around this. The **official JET website says** the following about TEFL certification:

Do I need TESL/TEFL certification to apply for the JET Programme?

TESL/TEFL certification is not a requirement for participation on the JET Programme but such certification will be an asset during the selection process.

As you can see, this is clearly an asset in applying for these highly competitive positions.

Kindergarten/International Pre-School

Although Junior High ALTs may have to smile and play with the kids, the preschool/kindergarten teachers can really expect to get a good workout. Stamina, cheer and lots of creativity are needed here, as you will be picking up kids, dealing with their emotional needs and making the class a fun and supportive place.

Many pre-schools hire native teachers who are expected to do a lot more than just teach English, though some regular Japanese kindergartens just hire an English teacher through dispatch companies to give the kids a feel for English. Pay can vary greatly by institution and position but the number of higher-paying international pre-schools is rising rapidly.

In those jobs, taking care of the kids along with lesson planning, gym activities and more is all on you. If you're looking for a challenge and love kids, then this is for you.

Pros:

- Much more room for personal career growth and creativity.

- Flexible schedule for part-timers.
- You can be a superstar to the kids and mums and a variety of activity in your day, *not boring.*

Cons:

- Barrier to entry can be high for full time positions that pay well (experience/qualifications).
- Lesson planning can be all on you, and you are sometimes responsible for all the kids (safety).
- Kids get sick so you need an awesome immune system or a lot of medicine from back home.

Qualifications needed:

Teaching experiences is almost always required. The vast majority require a teaching licence either from Japan or your home country, but some have managed to sneak their way in with a TEFL only. A teaching licence is really important when trying to get a good, high paying job at an international preschool. Not only will it qualify you for an interview (where you can show off your skills) but it will be invaluable for the actual teaching part, where you need to be using principles of language acquisition in your classroom teaching every day.

International Junior High/High School Teacher

The word "International" is used ever more in Japanese educational institutions, but only a handful are actually accredited international schools. These schools follow an international curriculum with high standards. Most are taught in English for all of the core subjects and, in some cases, using the local language for other subjects like gym or art.

Just as in the UK or the US, foreign languages like French or Spanish are offered and thus non-English natives have opportunities too. Pay and other benefits are the highest in the list thus far on average. Getting a placement as a teacher here is often possible from outside of Japan, but applying directly for international schools if you already live here is normal too.

Because of the high barrier to entry and great salary and benefits (by Japan's standards), few teachers leave these kinds of positions every year, so there aren't so many available. If you get a job offer to work at a real international school: don't blink, just go!

Pros:

- More responsible for your own work.
- Getting more involved in Japanese society and community.
- More opportunities to climb ladders in your career.
- Much higher pay opportunities.

Cons:

- More responsibilities (may require time investment after school and weekends for clubs, etc.)
- Time off not guaranteed always as deadlines must be kept for projects.

Qualifications needed:

These positions almost always require a teaching licence, preferably a Master's degree. Some teaching experience is also usually a must, as well as a very well crafted application.

Competition for these positions is very high, so it helps a lot to have a good network to give you a direct introduction to the school as these positions don't usually come up on job boards. These schools focus on candidates who have a teaching licence, and only having a TEFL course will at best separate you from other teachers by showing that you have understanding of how to apply those teaching skills to second language learning.

University Teaching

In terms of benefits, pay and time-off, nothing comes close to the University teaching positions. While International school teachers do well for themselves, university teachers can do just as well with only a few days a week teaching and all the holidays off.

An unfortunate trend in Japan now is to hire teachers into a separate department, technically not the university, and thus teachers there are offered fewer benefits. Japanese law allows the universities to consider lecturers as temporary employees for up to 5 years (which doesn't sound very temporary to me), but this may change in the near future as universities and government have had lots of bad press about this. Even in those cases this is still the highest paying, highest benefit job teaching in Japan.

Pros:

- High pay ratio to teaching time.
- Opportunities to teach at multiple institutions simultaneously.
- Much more involvement in planning own classroom curriculum, freedom to teach your way.

Cons:

- All responsibility for class is on the professor
- Very high barrier to entry. Networking and connections a big plus as positions are often not advertised. Often need to apply a year in advance.
- Qualifications needed and requires continued study.

Qualifications needed:

You will need a Master's degree in a related field and (paradoxically) it can be hard to get a job without experience teaching at university. How a TEFL qualification helps: University is one of the English teaching jobs in Japan where a TEFL course isn't all that valuable. Many of the teachers at these schools have master's degrees, PhD and doctorate level qualifications, so your TEFL course here will be ignored. Once you get your master's, look into getting more qualified with a PhD, getting some publications and making relationships with colleagues in your field to give yourself a boost into university teaching.

What you should expect/demand from your company while working in Japan

A "liveable" salary

You will see all kinds of jobs advertised in Japan, but I can tell you from experience that an absolute minimum payment you should expect is ¥240,000 per month. Any less and you may struggle to pay your bills or put anything into savings, and you can earn more than that even in entry level positions.

Charlie's first job in Japan at Peppy Kid's Club paid ¥250,000 per month (about $2500-3000 depending on exchange rates) from the start with no qualifications or experience. Many of the large companies will also help you find accommodation, which is welcome early on as startup costs for accommodation (頭金, *atamakin* - overhead costs) are usually very high. There are ways to limit this, and we talk about it in an **article** on our site about mistakes expats making when looking for apartments in Japan.

The school will make a profit from sub-letting you accommodation, so your monthly rent will be more than the apartment should be. Getting into your own apartment once you can afford it (and maybe once you change to a higher paying job) will give you some independence so you aren't relying on your company both for your job and your living arrangement and save you money in the long run.

Some companies that have raised red flags with foreigners in the past include Heart and Nova, so make sure you do your research and don't get screwed by bad companies that have a reputation. Heart just flat pays too low and offers little to no visa support. As we mentioned before, Nova got its bad reputation when they filed for bankruptcy and didn't pay many of the English teachers for months of work.

How much money should I be making in Japan after a year?

What you should be aiming for, after using this guide and the strategies we recommend, is **a minimum salary of ¥270,000 per month**. Your position should include company contributions for health insurance and pension as well as an end of year bonus of at least ¥100,000 in 1 year contract terms so you can re-negotiate at the end of the year to get more money or holiday time.

This should allow you to save, pay off student loans from back home if you have them, and enjoy going out with your friends without having to worry too much about being able to pay for your lifestyle. There are ways to get more than that, and getting a TEFL course along with the right teaching experience helped Charlie earn ¥320,000 a month with ¥400,000 in annual bonuses after only two and a half years in Japan.

Your company should do your basic income tax for you

Part of the reason for this is because Japanese taxes can be more confusing and expensive than you might expect, and paying it all in one go can be a big hurt if you're not prepared for it.

It is much easier if your company submits the tax return for you while taking it straight from your paycheck. If you have to do it yourself don't worry as you can do this at your local municipal tax office, but ask your company if they do it from the start like they should. Make sure to check at the end of the year to see if you are entitled to any tax rebates - in many cases you are as some schools don't put much effort into the forms, and forget to ask you for the deductions for NHI (National Health Insurance) and pension contributions as well as travel expenses.

You company should pay your commute to and from work

Every company I have ever worked for in Japan pays travel expenses. They all should, it is absolutely standard over here and if your company doesn't offer you this for some reason, that's potentially leaving a lot of money on the table. Make sure you get travel allowance. A company that doesn't pay your commuting expenses or caps them at an amount far below what it costs you to get to work should be an automatic red flag.

There are a lot of companies around Japan and we can't warn

you about every single bad one. Don't be afraid to ask other foreigners in Japan about the companies you apply to and their reputation. Make up your own mind about them. One of the companies that Charlie worked for early on in his Japan career seemed very draconic, but now he realizes that they weren't so bad after seeing some other companies out there. Take advice with a pinch of salt, but do ask for it to avoid wasting your time in a company that is known to not help foreigners advance or build their career in Japan.

The Reality of your First Job in Japan

You may be filled with wonder and awe at the possibilities of coming to Japan. You'll take up Kendo (剣道 - wooden sword fighting) and have tons of Japanese friends and speak the language really well in just a year, right? Maybe you read a lot of stuff online about Japan and that coloured your expectations, but it is important to temper your expectations a bit until you've been here a little while, because I am not the only one who had a massive shock with my first job here.

My school was in an extremely rural location, Iizuka city in Fukuoka. The town was tiny! In fact the best part about it was the train station. It took over an hour to get to Hakata station in the city and actually do something fun, and the last train home was at 11:06, after which I couldn't get home. Not an ideal location.

The town was so rural that there was no IC scan card at the ticket gate...

A co-worker and friend of mine actually once tried to get a taxi home after a drunken night out and ended up paying 30,000 yen ($300+) to get home! I once slept in a 24h internet cafe just to have somewhere to sleep for a couple thousand yen while I was out with friends. Needless to say it wasn't ideal. I knew that I couldn't hack it in Japan if I was stuck in the middle of nowhere, with a schedule that took away my evenings and weekends and a lack of opportunities to advance. I had to switch it up fast!

You can get out of your initial contract

If you came to Japan with a big company, they are pretty used to foreigners leaving their employ. It's not great to not finish your contract and you may need to explain it at a later date (interview for another company) but if you're stuck in the middle of nowhere and not enjoying your Japan experience, it'll be much better for you to move to somewhere you'd rather be and get the best of what Japan has to offer. Just remember that when you quit your job you'll need to give at least a month of notice. Some companies ask for more but when I spoke to a legal consultant about my school's three month notice clause in the contract, she informed me that it was unenforceable and that all I needed to give was 30 days. As usual with all legal information you find here or anywhere on the internet, check it for yourself. These things are prone to change regularly and I can't guarantee that this is still true whenever you are reading this, so be sure to talk to a free lawyer at your country's embassy or talk to Hello Work (Japan's working rights watchdog) if you need to check this.

So I handed in my notice 9 months after coming to Fukuoka, and moved on to the next thing. For me that ended up being Nagoya, where I got a job as an ALT, or Assistant Language Teacher. We'll talk about what that is in the section below on types of teaching jobs, but basically I was a teaching assistant in an inner city junior high school. Your first job in Japan can be a big shock, and completely not what you expect, but remember that the important thing is that you made it to Japan, and once you have your visa in hand you can start approaching other employers and looking for other jobs that will be more your style, in a place you want to be.

Before you hit the jobs boards looking for a way out, there are a few terms you'll need to understand. Like every other job, teaching has its own set of jargon to know, and in Japan there are a few others you'll need to be aware of.

Abbreviations used in Japan

Japan is seriously obsessed with shortening words and

making them quicker and easier to say. This applies to so many things, but don't think that because you're teaching English or working as a foreigner in Japan that you will be spared having to learn some abbreviations to get by here. Just think of one of Japan's most popular exports, Pokémon! It is a typical Japanese style shortening of the words 'pocket' and 'monster'. Some other fun examples include:

プリクラ - Purikura, short for プリントクラブ. These are arcade size machines that allow you and your friends to take weird and fun pictures together. Often they have what they call "beautifying" filters that make your skin shiny and clear and your eyes slightly bigger. Definitely try one with your friends for a laugh.

セクハラ - Seku Hara is short for sexual harassment. Don't do anything that could get you accused of this at work!

For English teachers, these are some of the abbreviations you'll hear a lot:

TEFL: Teaching English as a Foreign Language

Generally the term TEFL refers to a type of certification for teaching. A TEFL qualification is really the most efficient way to raise your income without going all-in on a Master's degree. They legitimise your application to any job as an English teacher, and definitely make you stand out more than the average foreigner in Japan.

TESL: Teaching English as a Second Language

TESL also often refers to a certification, or more often a master's program that qualifies you to teach English as second language, usually in English speaking countries.

ESL: English as a Second Language

This is by far the most common term you will learn as it relates to everything you as a prospective English teacher will be doing. Go to Google and start matching this term, "ESL" with others like "ESL Japan," "ESL advice," "ESL certifications," "ESL games" "ESL jobs," etc.

TESOL: Teaching English to Speakers of Other Languages

TESOL is often used more in academic settings. TESOL does not always refer to a certification or qualification so much as background in linguistics, teaching methodology and other concepts that relate to the field. It is more about the research done in the field of teaching English as a foreign language/second language and less about a TEFL/TESL like qualification. Thus, you often see a master's course in TESOL at universities.

CELTA: Certificate in Teaching English to Speakers of Other Languages

A slightly more advanced version of a TEFL course, but this one is accredited by Cambridge university, tends to be harder and is a stronger certification on your resume or CV than a TEFL course. Also tend to be significantly more expensive.

I wouldn't fret too much over one or the other or which one is more valuable as all of them prove you have an academic interest in teaching English, which is what you need to set yourself apart from other English teachers in Japan.

ALT: Assistant Language Teacher

An ALT is someone who helps the Japanese native staff in

the classroom to teach English with native sounding words. We will explain more about this job later, but in general ALTs work in junior high and high schools to help students build enough English knowledge to pass high school and university entrance examinations.

英会話: Eikaiwa

We covered this in other parts of the book, but in kanji this literally means, English and Conversation. So these tend to be English conversation schools, either in business districts for easy access to business people or schools for all ages of kids as an after school or weekend class. So you could say you are an 英会話教師 *Eikaiwa Kyoshi* "English conversation teacher."

There are also:

法会話 - *Houkaiwa* French

中会話 - *Chuukaiwa* Chinese (usually Mandarin)

西会話 - *Seikaiwa* Spanish

独会話 - *Dokukaiwa* German

If you are a native speaker of any of those languages above or know them to a decent level, I would do some Google searches with those words. There is a high chance that you can come up with a new job or side income opportunity teaching those languages, with much less competition than English teaching jobs might have.

There are a lot more words to know, of course, when teaching in Japan, but we will address the relevant ones as we progress through the book.

How Can You Build Your Resume to Get The Best-Paying Jobs Teaching English in Japan?

Rewind to my second year in Japan: I was struggling to find a way to get better paid jobs while teaching as an ALT in Nagoya. Everything I saw on GaijinPot was a big company with low/average pay looking for eikaiwa and ALT dispatch teachers. A lot of people really enjoy teaching at junior high, but it wasn't for me.

I had honestly thought about leaving Japan several times after just eighteen months here. When I had finished particularly bad days (silence in all of my second year classes made me question being a teacher at all) I knew that teaching teenagers was not for me. Nobody had told me how to get paid more or how to find jobs that were more fulfilling than just working a certain number of hours for a certain monthly salary.

After starting my meetup group in Nagoya, I quickly realized that I wasn't alone in this. I would say that maybe half of all of the teachers I met were not happy with the amount of pay they were getting.

While ¥250,000 is enough to survive on, it doesn't give you what you need to really feel happy about your job and your income. Even my little brother back home in the UK was making more money than me working in a repair shop. Good for him, you know, but I felt like I needed to be making much more to set myself up.

I wanted to be going out and having fun with my friends, going on holidays and making enough that I could afford to take a plane home for Christmas without asking my parents for help to pay for it.

My network and a great resume set me on the path to a massive increase in salary.

A very close friend of mine told me about a position in an international preschool. He knew someone working there and knew that they would be looking for a new teacher soon, but hadn't started to advertise the position yet. I sent them a resume and a well-worded cover letter asking for an interview.

What I didn't realize at the time was just how powerful this technique was.

Imagine you are a hiring manager at a school and you need to find a way to get a good teacher for your challenging educational environment, and the only places you know to find them are GaijinPot, Ohayo Sensei and Jobs in Japan. Lots of companies will be advertising on those platforms around that time (January and February are prime time for job applications for the new school year), so there would be a large number of resumes to read through for any job posting at that time.

Then before you spend the tens of thousands of yen it takes to put a job advertisement somewhere, a perfect (or near perfect) candidate with a TEFL qualification and 18 months teaching experience in Japan comes out of nowhere and hands you a solution on a silver platter. There is literally no downside to giving them an interview! Not only has the candidate proven themselves a go getter, but if they fit the job they have saved you a fair bit of money in advertising. If they aren't good enough for the job, then you can just continue advertising like you were intending to do anyway. It's a win-win and a no-brainer to give the interview.

So I got the interview as a homeroom teacher at the international preschool that I definitely wasn't ready for, but in the course of that year at the school I learned so much and because a much much better teacher. There are a ton of strategies that I (sometimes unwittingly) used to go on and raise my income from the starting Peppy Kid's Club salary of ¥250,000 per month to a much more respectable ¥280,000, and these same strategies worked when I moved on to a world famous school in 2015 paying ¥320,000 per month with ¥400,000 per year in bonuses that scaled up every year I stayed. Here we'll talk about some of the ways to craft your resume to get those jobs.

First thing you need to do is create a narrative for your resume

For most jobs you won't get far without having a well-crafted resume that leads to getting that interview. **Narrative** is the name of the game here. When people read your resume or cover letter you need to tell them a story. You want them to immediately think of you as the "teacher guy" or "teacher girl". Here is a principle to live by when it comes to resume writing:

If it doesn't earn its way on the page, it doesn't go on the page.

Your summer job at 'whole foods' when you were in high school isn't useful information for a teaching position, so it's not worth wasting space on.

Curated Education section - explain yourself

You might think that your education section can be the most boring part of your resume but I have had comments on this section in almost every job interview I've had in the past three years. This is because I put in my **academic interests** from when I was at university and now based on what I studied. It's very simple and it will get people more interested in you because you show your actual interests, which people can relate to more than just the title of your degree.

For example, rather than just saying "University of Warwick, UK" and leaving it at that, instead I put:

"University of Warwick, UK. **Academic interests include**: Developmental Psychology, Education, Learning methods, Persuasion, Debate and Logic."

So much better, isn't it? This shows any hiring manager that I'm interested in the academics of relevant skills for teaching. This part of a resume almost always has a comment in an interview, and I would argue that it helps to get the interview in the first place.

Work history - play up the <u>relevant</u> work

Recent graduates beware, putting every 2 week internship with long explanations on your resume will detract from your message. Remember that you want to be the "English teacher" not the "hasn't done much of anything and is trying to hide it" candidate.

Immediately you should take out the odd retail jobs you did in high school or relegate them to an "Other Jobs" section at the bottom. Then all of the jobs or work experience you have had that compliments a teaching position should be lightly explained. This shouldn't just be responsibilities; craft a two sentence story about what you loved about the job or what you learned.

Remember, you are trying to reach a human being and make them curious about you. Even babysitting for your aunt could be relevant if you are applying to work at a preschool or elementary school.

Inspiration to come to Japan - job, project, internship

"Why did you come to Japan?"

This is probably the second most common question you will be asked by Japanese people, right after "Where are you from?" Give it some real thought.

What is special about Japan that made you want to come here, of all places. A Japanese hiring manager doesn't want to hear that you came here because you couldn't get a job back home because of the economy. If Japan inspires you, you should say so. People love to hear from people who are inspired and happy to be where they are, especially in a job application.

Skills that are useful in the job

I'm sure everyone will be thrilled that you like music and hanging out with your friends, but rather than an interests or hobbies section, a skills section is much more useful on your resume. Ability to use computers, evidence of prioritising skills (with examples if necessary) and ability to work with others (this one is critical in most, if not all teaching environments in Japan. These are especially important when you're applying to work in a team environment like at a preschool (where you will likely team-teach with a Japanese native) or in an ALT position where you'll be working with others.

This is also the part where you put your Japanese ability. You don't want to leave this to a question at interview, especially if your Japanese level is very low. If you don't speak Japanese well, be up front about it so that it doesn't hurt your chances at interview. Better yet, start studying and pass the *Japanese Language Proficiency Test (JLPT) at level N5 or N4* to show that you at least have interest in learning to speak the language of the country you're living in.

Top tip: use this part to <u>checkbox the exact job specifications</u> from the job description. If the school asks for "at least *two years* teaching experience in high schools or junior high in Japan" then you can put "**three years** experience teaching experience in high school and junior high in Japan" right there in your skills section (if you have gotten to that point). Then when a hiring manager is going over it they will see that you have exactly what they need.

Slow down, take your time writing your resume.

There is usually time to put more effort into your individual applications. Make sure that before you submit that you have done everything you can to show the company that you are the right person for the job and that you have everything they are looking for.

Specifically rewrite your statements and even your resume for every job you go for. Personalise it for the job they are offering and you can get a great deal of success! You will look like you wrote your whole application just to get the job they are offering.

While resume writing can help you to get in front of a hiring manager, you will need to have a resume that at least has the requirements they need to fill. They are looking for great teachers who will get the job done, so you'll need to have a resume that has the substance to show that you can do that. Once you have an interview, you'll have a real chance to shine.

Get some resume templates that have worked for us at liveworkplayjapan.com/teach-english.

Interview Skills

Building interview skills are a massive life skill and much more than we can possibly go in depth into here. If you struggle with the interview process, you're going to struggle with getting jobs here in Japan as this is the most important part of the jobs process for Japanese companies.

It seems incredibly unfair, right? The job description doesn't say "interviewing" under daily responsibilities. That doesn't matter, unfortunately. You might be the best teacher in the world, but **if your interview skills aren't up to par then you won't get the job.** There are ways to work on this and a lot of personal development to do, but I'm going to give you the hacks I've used to get job offers at almost every interview I've had in Japan.

Confidence

Do you know how you can give yourself some confidence before a job interview? **Prepare for it, a lot!** Not just preparing materials and answers to questions, but mentally getting ready to get the job.

Be knowledgeable. Would you forget what to do next during a class? Well, er... It happens, but you don't want them to think that! There is a ton of psychology about confidence out there, but here is a quick list of things you can do to know what you're talking about.

You can be so well prepared that you don't need to worry about what they are going to ask. You have a core principle as a teacher and all answers will correspond to that. You have already rehearsed answers to the most common questions like:

"Why do you want to teach English (in Japan)?"

"What do you like about teaching English to [adults/high school kids/kindergarten kids]?"

"How would you plan a lesson for a class of quiet or shy kids?"

Being ready for this stuff will calm you down and you won't need to panic or worry when you get asked to explain yourself.

You also need to believe in yourself – it sounds corny to believe in yourself but you're going to be standing up in front of twenty, thirty, even forty kids every day and teaching them English while also making them laugh and have fun. You're good at this, don't forget that.

You also need to know, up-front, that you are a good fit for the job. If you're just applying because you need the job, you know that even a passably competent interviewer would be able to tell quite easily. If you applied for a job you didn't want, this will probably be obvious at interview. To combat this (especially if you actually do just need a job), coming across like a passionate teacher is going to be huge for your chances (more on this later).

You solve their problem

This is a principle of marketing that everyone should know, but few actually apply. They are a school with a "lack of teacher" problem, and you are a teacher with a "lack of school" problem. You just need to show them that you solve their problem in the best way possible.

Really know what you want out of the job and, more importantly, what that company wants and needs from you. What is their need that they're looking to fulfil by hiring you? They want to know that they are hiring a good teacher, and someone that can reliably do the job. You have to be polite, as appearance is a massive part of teaching in Japan. You will be talking to the parents in a lot of the school environments you get into, so being respectful (and better, speaking some Japanese) is important to show.

Bow properly and introduce yourself in Japanese at the start of the interview. This will show them that you can at least be communicative with other staff in Japanese, which is very helpful even if it isn't specifically required in your job.

When I had my interview at a world famous kindergarten, I actually started in Japanese by introducing myself. Then the directors continued in Japanese with me replying in Japanese for more than 20 minutes until they had some complicated contract questions that were a bit beyond my level, at which point the interpreter stepped in to help me out. This kind of thing will almost always impress a hiring manager because then they can have some faith that you can communicate without them needing to have an interpreter around for every little thing.

This is just one example but really it is worth taking the time to jot down what the company might want from its teachers. Responsibility, punctuality (for God's sake show up on time, **punctuality is a Japanese cultural point**) and enthusiasm are all big, but also think about what a Japanese company hiring English teachers wants.

Talk passionately about your students

There is nothing that will help you to get a job more than being emotive when talking about your teaching experience. Don't only talk about what it means to you, but what benefit the kids gain from having you as a teacher. It never hurts to talk about research you have done, so make sure you have read some recent studies about teaching methods and how people learn language.

Doing an online TEFL course will help you to have a few basic strategies and methods to call on when asked, but I like to read modern research coming out so I have something up to date to talk about in an interview. Where possible I like to talk about teaching methods that I have interest in, such as Montessori and science that I've read. I make it relatable to the kids that I would be teaching. Even past experience confirming that can really help make you seem like the best kind of teacher.

"I had this student who wouldn't say anything... then I tried asking them about their life and suddenly they were so talkative."

"I taught in a school and it seemed like all the kids were bored with the curriculum so I... arranging the class in Montessori style allowed the kids to have freedom and learn to..."

You can finish these kinds of sentences with your own stories. People can tell that I am a passionate teacher because of the way I talk about my students, with a big smile and lots of pride. I've gotten job offers on the spot because I talk so passionately about my students, how effective some of my lessons have been and how rewarding it was for me to help them get through some tough materials. Passionate teachers make good teachers, and while that isn't always the top priority in some schools in Japan, it definitely is for top performing schools that pay you better.

Impress them with your teaching demo

The part of the interview that a lot of my teacher friends hate is the dreaded demo. The demo is where the company will ask you to pretend that they, the interviewers, are children and teach them English in the kind of style you would if you were doing the job. It's nerve wracking and you might feel really silly for talking kindly and slowly to grown men pretending to be young students. Don't let it bother you, because the demo is actually the biggest opportunity you have to instantly put yourself in the running for the job.

Really this is key, most companies will hire or reject you in large part based on what they think of your demo. Typically a company will ask you to prepare a 5-20 minute demo to example teach (act out) for them in the interview room. Once I got to do the lesson with actual kids at the school, which is much much better, but this is very uncommon. Plan for ten minutes longer than they ask you to demo for just in case you are nervous and rush through all of your materials.

Another thing you really should do is prepare a quick paper copy of your demo preparation. This is important to show the school that you are able to create a lesson plan and follow it, with thought-out objectives and goals for the students.

Have your own questions

If you have no questions for a hiring manager at a job, there is a high likelihood that you won't get a job offer. It shows that you have no initiative, and that you don't care enough about the job to learn more about it.

You have to sell them that you can do the job, and if you show up reacting to what they say and thinking that canned answers to questions like "Where do you see yourself in five years" are gonna cut it, you'd be dead wrong! I've only once been asked that question in Japan, probably because most teachers only stay for a few years. They don't expect you to stay for five years.

They do expect you to care about the quality of work you do. Here are a few questions I think about before I go to an interview, and usually ask two or three of them.

- If I got the job, what would the average day look like?
- How many students are in the average class?
- I like to draw pictures and make extra materials for the students – how much freedom is there to do that within your curriculum?
- Do I get opportunities to come to kids' sports club games? (I went to maybe three club games at the Junior High in the year and it was not only fun but well worth it to support the team and build relationships with students, so don't shy away from this just because it might take up a morning on your weekend)
- Can I eat lunch with the kids or do I need to eat in the teachers room? This is one of my personal favourite questions to ask, shows that you like spending time with the students, and any face-time with the foreign teacher is valuable for the school.

Good questions help hiring managers know that you are a

serious candidate and have an inquisitive mind, and will seek answers before making potentially costly mistakes.

Your resume and interview skills are incredibly important, but they aren't going to be enough on their own to get you in the door of some of the better institutions out there. While many teachers believe that only taking time out to do an expensive Master's degree will get you to the next step, there is actually a much quicker and easier way to boost your English teaching career.

Get Formal Training Teaching English

Getting qualified is a long-term route if you are serious about your teaching career. Teaching in Japan isn't just a holiday, it is a profession. If you wouldn't hire someone unqualified for a job you were in charge of, why should they do it in Japan?

There are lots of kinds of qualifications that schools will look for but in our research for this book we found that a 120+ hour TEFL qualification is the most efficient way to level up your career because it requires the least amount of time while still offering tangible rewards. Of course a CELTA, teaching licence or a Master's degree are much more valuable, but they also cost a heck of a lot more and may take years to complete. The opportunity cost here is also a big factor to consider. Taking a month to do a CELTA or years to do a Master's degree will give you huge opportunities, but if you aren't sure how long you want to teach English in Japan, investing that much time into a qualification could be a problem for you.

Imagine spending years studying for a qualification, then getting into a job that you realize you don't want to do in the long term. This is in contrast to spending a few hundred dollars and studying in your free time while living your life in Japan, for me this was the most efficient way and it might well be for you too. If you're really sure that you want to teach English in the long term, go ahead to the section about further qualifications on CELTA and Master's degrees.

There are a ton of TEFL courses out there, and before you start teaching English you'll be hit with marketing speak about how much value they give you, how you can demand higher pay and get better jobs that a TEFL course will give you. The TEFL is valuable and worth having, but by itself it will not guarantee you the higher paying jobs. Many of the courses you'll find online include teaching experience in a real classroom. The thing is that not all TEFL courses are the same, and some are even not considered by major employers, so it pays to do your research in advance. If you can do a course in person, that is probably the way to go, but if you are already in Japan teaching English, getting a course online will definitely help your resume and prove to employers that you've taken the time to invest in your career as an English teacher.

A TEFL course has value for teaching in Japan as it proves an ability to work through the academics of English teaching, but getting basic teaching experience inside Japan is a more important part of your resume. That's what Charlie did, and he picked up a TEFL qualification while working full time at a school. Japan seems to be unique in Asia for this, as most other Asian countries require at least an online certification in advance of getting a teaching job. Getting a course online is the easiest way, and it is totally doable with a little focussed study while working here in Japan.

Well-Known TEFL Courses

There are a ton of TEFL courses out there, so it can be incredibly confusing try to choose one in the absence of clear information about the quality of each course. Here is a short price comparison of the courses, and we have negotiated affiliate connections with each of these companies to offer a discount on our website at liveworkplayjapan.com/teach-english. Here is a breakdown of the prices for the most well known TEFL courses:

International TEFL and TESOL Training

(ITTT)

$340 (120-hour)

International TEFL Academy

(ITA)

$1395 (170-hour)

TEFL Online

by Bridge TEFL

$640 (120-hour)

The Cost

As you can see above, prices range from ~$300 to well over $1000, especially if it includes direct lectures as opposed to online videos or other teaching methods.

You might be thinking: *"I can't afford to pay this much for a TEFL course right now."*

While there is no right path for everyone, once I had my TEFL qualification my salary went up by hundreds of dollars *per month*. The course has paid for itself many times over because of the jobs I have been able to get by having a qualification on my resume. Without it most employers would look at me as a "holiday" English teacher, and by that

I mean a person who is on *holiday* in Japan using *English teaching* to pay for it. That might be fine for a low paying eikaiwa job, but probably not the kind of person you want to hire in a high-performance school. Lots of courses also have classroom time included, but as we mentioned, if you get a job at a dispatch or eikaiwa company in Japan you **will be paid to get basic experience** rather than having to pay for it.

Cost isn't always a guarantee of quality

Be wary of some courses that will try to sell you on their specific course and how much it adds to your resume and employability, and don't be fooled by companies that offer "guaranteed" job placements for you upon graduating. You don't need to pay a TEFL company to find you a job, especially since you already have the Smart Guide.

Many employers don't know the ins and outs of which TEFL providers have a good reputation, and while some of them might look it up, really it's about what you want to get out of it. Chances are if the course felt too easy and you didn't learn much, a lot of good employers will know it isn't worth the paper it's printed on.

Then why do I need a TEFL course?

For many positions in Japan, your TEFL certificate will be important. These often happen to be those that offer above average pay. While there are plenty of examples of teachers who are compensated quite well without the certificates, a TEFL can help tip the scales in your favor. Certification will help you to get out of the "English for cash" schools and catapult you to a better job. We believe that having a 100+ hour TEFL qualification is fantastic for showing the better schools that you have an academic interest and foundation in teaching English, not just speaking it. Having a TEFL course is not necessary for teaching in Japan, but it is valuable for getting the higher paying jobs.

Without at least a TEFL course you run the risk of being confused for one of the foreigners who are on holiday in Japan and only using English teaching to pay the bills.

Two major benefits:

1. Value differentiation in the market: You will out-qualify teachers with similar experience, especially in the first few years of your time in Japan. That way you will be more likely to get the job in the first place.

2. Higher paying jobs become more accessible: Jobs that give preference to TEFL certificate holders tend to have a higher salary. Just search on Jobs in Japan or GaijinPot for the keyword TEFL and see the average offered salary rise by 10-20% or more!

Quite simply, being qualified gives you higher chance to get a better job that pays more money.

I found that getting a TEFL qualification **online a year or two after I started teaching** gave me the best value. I paid about $400 for my qualification and now I have an accredited course on my resume. It has lent to my credibility as an English teacher and I use what I learned from it at school frequently when I explain why I am teaching the way I am.

There are tons of courses out there but some are more reputable than others. A lot of the cheap TEFL courses out there are just trying to get your money, and checking their accreditation will help you figure out which ones those are.

These courses are less likely to actually teach you anything, so while you might get the boost to the resume that we're talking about (with some uninformed companies), you might find that in the classroom you haven't had enough information to actually improve your teaching very much. This is essential too as getting recommendations from your school as a great teacher will really help you when applying for other jobs. Even if they don't ask to see your recommendations, these tell a story that will help you to connect with the hiring manager and get you into an interview.

"I read on the internet that TEFL is worthless."

This is just flat untrue, and people who say this are usually in one of two groups. Either they don't have a TEFL (or have a disreputable one) and don't want to invest in themselves, or they have a TEFL but don't have the job search skills to leverage it properly. We did research, and checked hundreds of jobs on the internet. Even a quick search of GaijinPot and Jobs in Japan found that companies that required TEFL or preferred TEFL certificate holders had much higher starting salaries, and were generally speaking more favourable positions. Check out these ones we found in a quick search.

Higher paying schools where TEFL is recommended or required:

My English school has a requirement of a TEFL qualification, and offers a ¥260-270k to start. An easy level up from base eikaiwa salary.

学校法人 鶴学園

T S U R U   G A K U E N

Tsuru Gakuen in Hiroshima requires TEFL in addition to a teaching licence, and boasts an exceptional ¥390k a month salary! They are even willing to sponsor your visa. Nice!

SHANE
ENGLISH SCHOOL

Shane English School has a strong preference for TEFL holders and offers an above average 15k a day, or 300k a month at an average 20 day schedule.

NES Language schools offers up to ¥350,000 for teachers who have a TEFL, TESOL or CELTA.

ESP Japan offers corporate English teaching jobs paying ¥290-300k per month for teachers with a TEFL.

None of these schools are partners of ours - these are just examples of well paying jobs that require a TEFL qualification.

How do I know which TEFL course is good enough?

I took a 150 hour Master's course with TEFLUK that gave me some strong foundations in education theory and definitely helps me to get all kinds of jobs that my experience alone might not always qualify me for. It was fairly good with a lot of content but some of the lessons felt a little rushed. Some of the videos were very dry and not engaging to watch, and some of the teachers they used for the video examples were a little irritating and I wouldn't want to teach like that.

It really depends on your budget which course you might take. For those who just want a little extra information before coming to Japan, a cheaper course might be all you need to give you some confidence starting out as a new teacher here. However it is important to bear in mind that a lot of employers know which courses are cheap certification mills and which ones are legitimate qualifications. If it seems really cheap, it's probably because it isn't a great course and won't teach you enough to be worth it for an employer to consider. If your budget can afford it, the ITA course is widely respected, but there are other courses out there and if you are still in your home country and have time before coming to Japan, a course with in-class experience is highly recommended. If you're already in Japan, save up and get the most respected course you can. As usual, double check with your own research, being sure to listen to what employers in Japan are looking for.

For non-native speakers of English

To tell you that where you are from doesn't matter would simply be inaccurate. It can be a disadvantage, but don't let that keep you down. Martin has worked in Tokyo teaching English with colleagues from the Philippines, Malaysia and Singapore. Charlie has many friends from Indonesia, Belgium and Hong Kong working in high-end ESL jobs at private schools in Japan. No matter where you are from, if you have great English skills and the qualifications to back them up you can find great jobs in Japan.

Let's be clear: If you are a non-native speaker of English or if you come from a nation where English is not the only language spoken such as Malaysia or India, you will still have opportunities to teach English in Japan, but it will be harder and you will need to be ready to prove your English skill. It will be harder for you to find competitive ESL jobs than people from nations like the UK and the US. Japanese people tend to be better at written English as well, so they might test you. If your spelling or grammar aren't up to par, this will be a problem for you trying to get jobs teaching English in Japan. Becoming TEFL certified will certainly tip the scale in your favour and give you some very useful advanced grammar guidance that even native speakers find useful for explaining our crazy language.

Successful Non-Native English Teachers

Nicholas S. (Indonesia)

"I came to Japan on a tourist visa and got a job on the ground here. I'm not going to lie, being a non-native speaker is a disadvantage, but if you have qualifications you can get awesome jobs where they aren't just looking for a stereotype and will pay well for a good teacher."

Thomas P. (Belgium)

"I hold some qualifications including a Master's in Communication and an ITA TEFL course. When I arrived in Japan I immediately started sending out resumes to all schools I could find. My rule was 10 schools per day, so very quickly I had applied to over 100 schools. Most of them asked for people who already have a visa, but one needed someone ASAP. They gave me the job and sponsored my work visa, and the rest is history!"

Being certified in TEFL by a well-known, internationally accredited brand will be all the more important for those who do not come from countries where English is a national language. A TEFL and a little extra hustle will help make sure you can secure your first well paying ESL job in Japan.

Something to note: In Japan the TOEIC has become the gold standard for English language testing, so if you take this test and get a high TOEIC score of at least in the 900s, you'll find Japanese employers will be impressed and you will find it easier to score those high-paying jobs.

Teachers with TEFL qualifications in Japan:

Taylor

"The TEFL course was great preparation for my class. I still refer back to lesson plans and activities I did throughout the course when planning activities and assignments for my students."

Meredith

"I took the Cambridge CELTA course... and got a job teaching in Japan through AEON, one of the biggest English conversation schools in the country. Now I live and teach in beautiful Inuyama, a city of about 75,000 people 30 minutes away from Nagoya."

Kaye

"It's important to keep in mind that schools here are looking for a lot more than just a TEFL certificate, too. Aside from the basic credentials, your history and personality take you a long way. My experience living abroad, Japanese studies, TEFL background, and my can-do attitude made me an ideal candidate."

Next Level Qualifications

CELTA: The Certificate of English Language Teaching to Adults

CELTA's are basically **a TEFL course on steroids**. It is similar to a TEFL but accredited by Cambridge University in the UK. You can take CELTA courses all over the world but only with a university; they are highly respected as a teaching qualification in Japan. Usually the certificate takes the form of a 120 hour or more in-person intensive course and even for the value it provides, a CELTA will cost you. The course fees on Teaching House, a Cambridge University partner in providing CELTA, is $200 for enrollment and then the course itself will cost $2,495. Those fees are standard. Even in places where these courses are cheaper, by the time you pay for travel and living expenses, it might end up still being cheaper to get your CELTA in the US, the UK, Australia or your nearest CELTA providing country.

A CELTA is more respected and of greater value than a TEFL by all accounts, but remember that a TEFL is all you will need to get lots of the higher paying jobs in Japan and in other countries too. If you can afford the course fees and the time, a CELTA is a top qualification you should be looking at unless you have plans to get a teaching licence or Master's degree.

Teaching Licence

This might take a year or more and may require you to return to your home country and get your qualification there. I'm from the UK and our PGCE programs allow students to become qualified teachers in a one year master's style program with teaching experience and study. Other countries are different, but it isn't too much work to check which colleges offer these courses of study. Below is some information for the major English speaking countries – direct links will be on liveworkplayjapan.com/teach-english.

USA

Eligibility: https://www.teach.org/teaching-certification

Institutions offering PGCE courses in the USA: http://www.hotcoursesabroad.com/study/training-degrees/us-usa/teacher-training-courses/loc/211/cgory/o3-3/sin/ct/programs.html

Getting Certified: https://www.teachforamerica.org/join-tfa/leading-classroom/training-support/getting-certified

UK

PGCE: https://www.prospects.ac.uk/postgraduate-study/teacher-training/pgce

Qualified Teacher Status: https://www.gov.uk/government/collections/qualified-teacher-status-qts

Australia

Information: http://www.aitsl.edu.au/

Canada

Eligibility: https://www.bcteacherregulation.ca/teacher/InternationalGraduates.aspx

Institutions offering PGCE courses in Canada:

http://www.hotcoursesabroad.com/study/training-degrees/canada/teacher-training-courses/loc/32/cgory/o3-3/sin/ct/programs.html

There are a limited number of universities in Japan with links to universities abroad that offer courses for aspiring teachers to get their actual teaching licence. There's one at Osaka University, and others can be found in your local area with a Google search. Just be sure to note the difference between a teaching licence and a TEFL/TESOL course. A teaching licence allows you to teach at international and prestigious private schools, a TEFL/TESOL course generally speaking would not.

Master's Degree and above

This one is most likely the biggest time and money investment, but helps you get the option to teach at the university level. Lots of teachers I have met in Japan want to teach at a university, but getting that master's qualification is a pretty big first step. It's costly and can take years to train for, is highly academic and just plain difficult.

I know a few university lecturers and professors in Japan and there are a lot of benefits to getting to this stage, but you need to get your foot in the door first. **This doesn't always mean getting a master's degree** but to get there without one takes a lot of positioning, luck and talent. It can be done, but if teaching at this level is your goal then I wouldn't bank on it. Lucking into a university teaching position is the tiny exception to the generally hard and fast rule that you need a Master's qualification and preferably experience teaching at a university.

That's a pretty paradoxical barrier, huh? Getting university level teaching experience is hard to get if you don't already have university teaching experience! This is where networking can be a big part of your job search (more on that later).

Temple University in Tokyo and Osaka is one institution in Japan to get your Master's, but there are many others and it all depends on what you are looking for and your own situation.

Take a look around at the universities in your local area and the ones that offer distance learning. It's a tough step, but if you want to be a university teacher and make the big bucks then you'll need to think about doing this.

Methods and strategies to get the best jobs in Japan

Most people have no idea what they need to do to get a good job here in Japan. And why would they? After all, the vast majority of foreigners who move here don't speak any Japanese and got their first job in Japan while they were overseas. Once you get to Japan though, the whole market opens up and you need to know what resources and methods there are to get a job here.

Of course the first stop for most people in the modern world are the jobs boards. As far as we are concerned these should be just the start of your job search toolkit, and once you have built up your resume and your network, these will take a backseat. While there are occasionally some good jobs on here, the competition is high and the rates are industry standard or even lower than you would get if you knew how to do a better approach.

This is true across the board when finding work in Japan. Here is a map of Charlie's teaching career in Japan, and just notice how much the rate goes up as the method of search changes. Going from looking on jobs boards and hoping something nice comes up to using your network and applying directly, there is an obvious link.

非公開の求人案件 - Secret Job Listings

Hikoukai no kyujin anken

In the Japanese career world, the vast majority of job

openings are referred to as 非公開 *Hikoukai*. This means that they are not publicly listed anywhere online. They are only known about internally and shared with select parties like recruitment firms or larger ESL companies such as Aeon or Berlitz.

You may want to bypass middleman companies like these. The way to do that is go directly to a school board or the company, or have a strong enough network that people will tell you when they hear of an opportunity. Sometimes it is a matter of timing. The big hiring seasons in Japan are the months prior to financial and school year beginning April (Mid January ~ end of March) and for international academies in September (Mid June ~ end of August).

With the tactics we'll talk about in this chapter, you can get direct access to the 非公開 *Hikoukai* positions. Negotiating for yourself won't be as easy and it will seem less safe than just getting a job at a bigger company, but once you start doing it you'll be earning more money without middlemen taking their share, and you'll have learned and mastered the valuable life skill of self-promotion.

Get as Long of a Visa Term as Possible

Visa terms come in one, three and five year terms for the working visas. It is really important to give your visa application the best chance of having a long period of stay, with at least three years being ideal. For any expats who are married to a Japanese national, this will not be a problem as the renewal is a rubber stamp. For the rest of us, we usually are started off with a short term one year visa, which can be a pain as you have to go through the arduous process of renewing again, and it can affect the kinds of jobs that you can get. Some companies don't like the idea of hiring someone whose visa application they may have to support the following year.

Unfortunately it seems almost completely random whether you get a long term visa or a single year extension. Three people working at my school last year all came to Japan at the same time and worked for the same company, but the Americans both got a one year extension and the British guy got a three year extension, even though they work for the same company. I have seen the same thing with the nationalities reversed, so it doesn't seem to correspond to where the person comes from.

Some lawyers will try to convince you that they can ensure that you get a three year visa if you pay them ¥40,000 or so, but they absolutely can't. It is completely up to the whims of whichever immigration officer reviews your case, and the only thing that you can do in the application phase to have a higher chance of getting the three year visa is to get the company to submit a separate form with details of their company to sponsor your visa renewal. Do this if you can.

Having a long term visa kept Martin in Japan

Martin got his first job in Japan working at an international kindergarten. He met his mentor, a university English professor while studying abroad in Japan. That same mentor happened to be on the board of directors of the NPO that runs the school.

It was only later that Martin happened upon the school and applied without knowing that his mentor was on the board of the school. *It really helps to have contacts even if you never know how they might help you in the future.* He just found the school listed on an old website called Tokyo with Kids. Martin worked at the school for a year, and while the opportunity wasn't the right fit for him, thankfully Martin had two years left on his visa and could seek out other opportunities without needing to have a job in hand to stay here.

If Martin only had a one year visa, he would have had to get a new job immediately to support his visa extension. Rushing into a job just to get visa support makes it hard to find work that takes you where you want to go.

Charlie focussed most of his work in Japan on English teaching, moving up the pay-scale with every new position he took. This is a plot of Charlie's path:

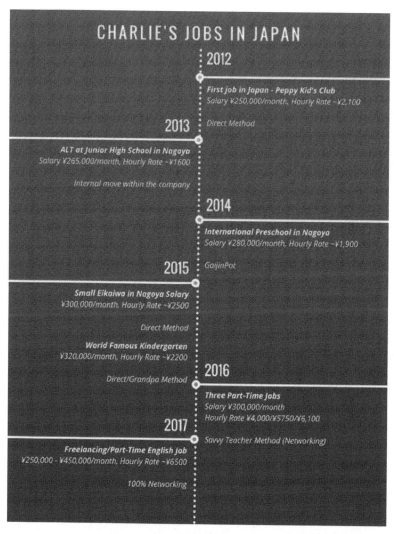

CHARLIE'S JOBS IN JAPAN

2012

First job in Japan - Peppy Kid's Club
Salary ¥250,000/month, Hourly Rate ~¥2,100

Direct Method

2013

ALT at Junior High School in Nagoya
Salary ¥265,000/month, Hourly Rate ~¥1600

Internal move within the company

2014

International Preschool in Nagoya
Salary ¥280,000/month, Hourly Rate ~¥1,900

GaijinPot

2015

Small Eikaiwa in Nagoya Salary
¥300,000/month, Hourly Rate ~¥2500

Direct Method

World Famous Kindergarten
¥320,000/month, Hourly Rate ~¥2200

Direct/Grandpa Method

2016

Three Part-Time Jobs
Salary ¥300,000/month
Hourly Rate ¥4,000/¥5750/¥6,100

Savvy Teacher Method (Networking)

2017

Freelancing/Part-Time English Job
¥250,000 - ¥450,000/month, Hourly Rate ~¥6500

100% Networking

As you can see, the riskier and less competitive the method, the higher the pay and more interesting the job. The jobs picked up on jobs boards are a great start, but as you learn more and become a more capable teacher, you'll want to learn the valuable skills of direct application and using your network effectively. Let's start off with the jobs boards.

The Most Well Known Jobs Board – GaijinPot

GaijinPot

GaijinPot.com Jobs is the by far the most well known job board in Japan with likely the largest employment board for teaching jobs in Japan on the internet.

Having used GaijinPot for years, I can now say that I rarely use this job board for anything other than seeing where the standard rates are moving (and it isn't in the right direction). After being bought out by Fuji Media Holdings, GaijinPot has raised their prices for posting an ad by a LOT. This has all but shut out the smaller schools from advertising there, so mostly big eikaiwa companies offering the same standard rates post job ads here. This ad buy cost comes straight out of your salary, which is why companies that used to have competitive pay now are paying less than when I moved here in 2012.

When you first move here there are some options on this board for you. Everyone in Japan will say they use it, but you'll rarely see an English teaching job on here that pays more than ¥280,000 even in the heart of Tokyo. Once you have been in Japan for a year or two and have TEFL qualifications to prove your skills, you'll want to move on to the more powerful methods we start talking about below.

Pros:

- Great resource to learn what companies are out there, what positions exist and who is hiring.
- Guaranteed hiring companies listed. Mostly big legit companies as the cost to post an ad is pretty high.
- Easy to use with good search functionality and lots of job postings all through the year.

Cons:

- High competition = lower chances of getting a response from companies.
- Difficult to find positions with high salaries on the site due to the high supply of willing teachers and often insufficient demand for them.

- Your application is sent through a resume form rather than your own resume. This means your application will look just like everybody else's, with little space to differentiate yourself with the narrative we talked about earlier.

What we recommend:

We recommend you use the techniques we will outline and detail later to find higher paying jobs directly. This is especially true in Tokyo where you can earn a lot more than you'll likely ever find advertised on GaijinPot. GaijinPot is an excellent resource for getting **ideas and a general overlook** about what companies are out there and what the demand is like in the market, but it is a first stop, not the be-all and end-all.

One great use for GaijinPot and other job boards mentioned here is to use them to scout out companies. Then go call them or visit them directly with your resume in hand using the Grandpa Method we talk about later on. Your chances of landing an interview increase exponentially by doing this. If you can find schools directly to apply for before they put out a job ad, the company won't have to pay a fee to recruiters, which could go back into your salary. This requires some time in Japan and keeping your ear to the ground, as well as using the techniques we're going to talk about more below.

A indicator of how TEFL helps you: search for "TEFL" on GaijinPot as a keyword of a job search. As a general rule you will see the average salaries rise quite a bit.

JobsinJapan.com is a site that has been helping people find jobs here since 1998, and has been renewed recently under new management. It is starting to have a good selection of smaller schools with fewer employees, a place where good teachers can improve their skills and their salary as well. Definitely worth checking out!

While this board has actually been around for a long time, only recently with the help of former staff of G+ Media did it become a much more valuable ground for foreigners here in Japan. The price to post an ad here is much lower here than for many other job boards, so it is becoming a great place to find some of the smaller schools who will be more personable and less corporate. These are usually better places to learn and grow as a teacher and set you up to have better experiences for the future.

Pros:

- New jobs added throughout the year.
- For employers the cost to post an ad is much cheaper than GaijinPot, so you're more likely to find smaller schools than bigger faceless companies.
- You can apply with your own resume/CV as opposed to other websites filled forms. This is important, as those resume forms you have to fill out on other sites like GaijinPot stop you from standing out with your well crafted resume narrative we talked about before, and make you look just like everyone else.

Cons:

- Not as big as GaijinPot, so if you're just looking for something in your area there may be fewer jobs available.
- Search functions on the site are not as detailed as GaijinPot and it is harder to see at-a-glance relevant details about the job – you'll have to look through to the individual job pages for many details that you might prefer to see before clicking through.

O-HAYO SENSEI

Ohayosensei.com has a good list of teaching jobs throughout Japan, and is often a good place to find competitive or high-end jobs around Japan. I've seen teaching jobs on here paying ¥400,000 per month, which I would call exceedingly uncommon on a regular jobs board. The other main difference from GaijinPot and JobsinJapan is the layout. This is not an easy place to search, and Ctrl+F will be your friend here. This will open a "find word" tab in your browser, which you can use to search for keywords like the city you live in. It is a job board where you can just see available jobs in plain text, but sometimes there are surprising gems on here, so keep an eye out.

Some other job boards we have used:

Myshigoto: A job board for finding jobs in Japan.

Dave's ESL Cafe: This is for TEFL jobs mostly. You can not only apply for jobs but find institutes and online schools to get TEFL certified on this site.

Career Cross: Primarily for Japanese speakers but the English site is a good place to find all sorts of jobs in Japan and isn't limited to ESL jobs. You can often find English corporate teaching positions or higher paying ESL jobs through job boards like Career Cross.

ELT News: A great website for news on all things ELT. Click the link for the job board

TES: For certified teachers primarily but still a good place to look even if you are not certified. TES lists international schools, kindergartens and nursery schools as well as private schools. **TIE** is also a good place to find international schools positions in Japan, then apply by the direct method.

JACET: The Japan Association of College English Teachers. This job board is mostly in Japanese for colleges and universities in Japan.

Don't be scared if you cannot read Japanese to go through job listings on some of these sites. There are ways to get around it. One option would be to use Google translate, and another would be to hire a virtual assistant on Upwork to help you get through Japanese job listings and applications. This is better for the higher end, but if you pay someone even a few hundred dollars but you wind up landing a university job paying ¥500,000 or more a month, just think of what the return on investment that would be!

The Direct Method - Apply to the School

What did people used to do before there were online jobs boards? They would go directly to companies they wanted to work for and say: "I want to work for you." Sounds crazy right, but guess what? This method is much better than going through the jobs boards.

Role-play a hiring manager for a second and think about it. You haven't dropped a huge wad of cash on advertising for the position you need filled, but you're planning to in the future. Then out of nowhere someone messages you and says: "I found your school online and it looks amazing. I love how you did your young learners initiative to give the students more time to learn independently and help them set their own goals. I'd love to work at your school."

Doesn't that just sound like a much better introduction? Better than spending money on an advertisement and then having your email inbox inundated with hundreds of emails with long resumes and cover letters, this teacher seems passionate to work at this school. It's a win-win.

Think about how much higher your chances are to get an interview when you have shown initiative and complemented the school you are applying for in your first email to them. You're far and away a better candidate than the other people who are just reacting to a post on a jobs board, and you'll have done enough research to know something specific about the school that you can say good things about.

Step-by-step how to apply directly to schools.

First: you'll want to find a school that you like the look of and do some research. Look up the school's name in quotations in Google and see if there is any media about the school, any work they have done that is interesting or something special about the school. Don't be afraid to search the school name in Japanese and then use Google translate to give you English if you need it.

You can use the above list, a Google map search, an internet article or anything else to find schools. If there isn't anything special about it on the internet (in Japanese either), take a minute to think why this might be. They might just not be online or up front about their successes, or there might just not be that many good things about the school.

Find the school's website or contact info online and keep a note of it. If you are applying to multiple schools, remember to keep all of this information in a simple word doc or spreadsheet so you know what stage of the process you are at. If you go to a school and see the name of a person in a hiring capacity, you may be able to look up their phone number (at the school, not a personal number... that's creepy) and call them if you cannot find the email.

Best: email first with your resume and cover letter, then call them a short time after and tell them you emailed them.

If you call or email, it really helps to know the name of a key player or hiring manager in the school or company. Gate keepers do not like being emailed with resumes and don't know what to do with them. People in a position to employ you do like them and know what to do with them.

The most important thing is that you make the effort to put in some face-time. Talk to the person, make sure they know that you are a human being and not just another disembodied email taking up their time and attention. Talking on the phone or meeting in person is absolutely critical to getting a job using the direct method.

Pros:

- Apply to a school or company out of the job board system- this means you can be free to email them directly or if they have multiple emails, you can email all of the ones you find, instead of just what you find on Ohayo sensei or GaijinPot.
- You can apply to companies that do not list their job postings on the popular job boards, and they are more likely to invite you to interview due to the lower number of applicants.
- Salary - I'm sure you knew this already but advertisements on job boards cost money. What you might not have known is that the money spent advertising your position comes straight out of the budget for your salary. When you apply directly, you are able to ask for as much as 10% more than a position with a salary listed on a jobs board.

Cons:

- Takes more work to craft your CV. You have to spend some real time thinking about how to communicate with a specific school, and sometimes you get no response at all. This is uncommon with this method, but it does happen, so disappointment can be a factor here.
- Employers may not be expecting your application and the process may not go as smoothly as with the other companies or schools that advertise on the main job boards.

- They may not be expecting a call or email from an applicant in English. It may be necessary to use Japanese at some stage in applying to employers like this or, due to language barrier issues, it may take more time to talk to someone who has influence over hiring.

Email script for sending your resume over

Here is a resume script I've been using for years to apply for positions at schools in Japan. You don't have to follow it to the letter, but it is a good starting point from which you can refine it to your own liking.

For the attention of [name of hiring manager]

I recently came across [video, article, information or testimonial about the school and its teaching philosophy] and I thought that your school looks amazing / interesting / innovative.

I've been teaching in Japan [and overseas if applicable] for x years and I've rarely seen schools like yours that focus on [example: such well-rounded learning and not just academics/international qualifications and global initiatives/individual students well-being and not just a collective group].

I strongly believe in [your teaching principles that match the school's ideals here: for example: learning through play,

---

teaching children to be kind and caring, less academic study etc.].

I would love to be a part of your school. Are you hiring English teachers right now? I'd love to apply to work at your school.

I live in [somewhere] now but I would move [closer to your school] if I could work for you. [Add this if at all possible but this definitely made my application shine]

Please find my resume, cover letter and references attached.

Sincerely,

[name]

How much better is that than "I saw your job post on a jobs board. Give me a job please!"

For more email templates go to our resources section for this book at **liveworkplayjapan.com/teach-english**.

This takes a lot more work than the first two options as you have to craft your CV, cover letter and application to the school directly, and do some homework on them rather than just applying to everything within a 30 mile radius and hoping for the best. Some people say that applying for an English teaching job in Japan is a numbers game, but they are only partly right. Sure, applying to fifty schools might yield more chances than just applying to one, but if your application to that one school is deep and thought out, and it shows that you have passion for working there, and you'll put yourself in a good position not only to get the job but to have a chance at getting higher pay as well.

Using your TEFL qualification to boost your chances

Once I got my TEFL qualification, my next job paid ¥20,000 more per month, and then the same increase for two later jobs in Tokyo. One of those jobs paid ¥320,000 a month with an additional 400,000¥ of bonuses spread throughout the year. Undoubtedly years of teaching experience, a passion to work at this specific school and qualification in TEFL made a strong case for hireability.

In this circumstance it is essential that not only your application is incredible, but that you also interview very well. Be on time, polite, knowledgeable, passionate, friendly... basically be a great candidate. Use what we taught in the chapter about interview skills to make sure that if you do get past the gatekeepers, you actually have the best shot at getting the job in the end.

The Grandpa Method - Walk In And Get A Job

We have talked about this at length in our podcast with Marco, a friend of ours who put this method to good use in our high-stakes field test. The general idea that if you really need a job and you need it right now then go to private schools and smaller eikaiwas in your area with a CV, looking smart and ready to go, and you can get a job. Martin taught Marco how to do it and in a high stress situation, he used this to score a high paying job within a week!

This is just another tool in the toolbox that can allow you to find jobs that are not being advertised but that pay exceptionally well. This is especially true in the weeks leading up to the new school terms in April and September.

Imagine you are a hiring manager at a school, and you had someone for the job but they backed out at the last minute for a family emergency, for example. Now you have a week until the school starts and you are minus one English teacher! Then some guy walks in off the street, TEFL qualified and smart looking who can fill the role and help keep you from losing face in front of parents of students who are paying to have an English class. **You're going to take that option.**

This is what you do:

- Use our resume guide above to make sure your resume looks amazing.
- Print out any references you have from previous schools
- Look up private and international schools (public schools have procedures for hiring that may preclude this technique working) in the areas you would be willing to work and send the decision maker (find out who this is on the school's website) your resume by email the night before.
- Wake up in the morning and physically go to the school, dressed up professionally with a paper copy of your resume and ask to speak to the person you found at the school who makes the hiring decisions. Be super polite and warm. Smile.
- Talk to the person in charge of hiring and explain how you would love to work at their school.

We understand that it is scary to think of doing this, but don't make excuses for why it won't work. It works! This is the method your grandpa used to get his first steel mill job, or that your great grandpa used to work in the government office. Before Monster.com people would ask business owners if they could work for them. This is why we call it the Grandpa Method.

When you just fill out forms and send emails, you don't create a human connection with your potential employer. You just put more work on their plate, and the delete button is only a quarter-inch mouse move and a click away from being totally ignored. This method works for all kinds of people because it shows initiative, which business owners love to see in their employees.

Marco was born in Puerto Rico. You know how annoying it was for him to explain that to Japanese every time they asked, お国はどちらですか (where are you from)? There must have only been a handful of times anyone even knew where that was. This never stopped him from applying the *Grandpa Method*.

Marco started out teaching English to kids. His education was in Spanish teaching and that was what he really wanted to teach. He was patient. After he quit his job in Tokyo, with rent due in a matter of weeks, he hit the road and started applying to schools, then showing up with an extra copy of his resume, ready to start.

It didn't take months, it took days before job offers started coming in. He had choices, and turned down some jobs because he had such great responses using this method that he held out for something better. He wound up at a full time job with an international school teaching Spanish. It was his best paying job up to that point too, and let him do what he **wanted** to do rather than what he **had** to do to make rent.

He didn't get the job in a day, but he had been keeping his ear to the ground and was out and about in Tokyo making connections and showing up ready to do the job. I wish there was a formula to give you for every situation, but really you need to lay the groundwork with your connections and your reputation in the long run. Do the things above and stay positive. Keep on your mission. The right opportunities will come to you sooner or later, and if you use the Grandpa Method to get jobs that are never advertised on jobs boards, you can end up with higher pay than you might be used to.

The Savvy Teacher - Networking for Higher Paying Jobs

This one is a critical way to start rising above the rest and getting a much better pay from your skills in Japan. If you have been in Japan for a while you'll start to meet people. These people can get you jobs. I'm not talking about other just-here-for-a-break-from-real-life teachers who don't have a passion for education. Be friends with them, but definitely be on the lookout for people who have been in Japan for a long time and make friends with them.

Let me repeat that: your friends can get you jobs.

In the last two years of English teaching I have gotten all of my high-paying jobs through networking. After meeting a young entrepreneur who was running her own yoga school, I got a tip from her about an opening at a school her friend was working at. They were looking for a part time teacher in the mornings once a week, and the pay was ¥5,750 per hour! That's nearly triple the standard rate for English teachers.

While it was only four hours per week, in a month that made me nearly ¥100k richer and for only four teaching hours per week. The majority of English teachers in japan are working 30 or 40 hours per week to get their ¥250k. That doesn't need to be you.

Another job I got through my network was a spot teaching a specialised debate class at a private high school in Tokyo. The pay was the same as the last, ¥6,000 per hour, and for three classes per week.

With those two jobs alone I had ¥170k coming in, and for only about 10-12 hours of my time per week including the lessons themselves, travel and lesson planning. This is how your friends can help you, but not just any friends. If all of your friends are other teachers who are content with working their nine-to-five and living for the weekend, you won't get any opportunities from them. Meeting people doing interesting and challenging things in Japan is the best way to expand your real network and get jobs that are never put on the jobs boards.

How to find jobs through savvy teachers:

The first group of people you'll want to know are the long-term expats in Japan. Many of them may still have a hand in teaching, or know people who do. Great places to meet them are meetup events (business meetups, not party events) or at the part-time jobs you start to get if you're mixing and matching as I was. I actually met some of my best contacts working part-time, as the other people I knew were also doing the same thing. One of them is working for four schools at once, three of which are university run high schools, and has incredible holidays (I'm actually jealous) and a year round salary of over ¥400k a month, even when he isn't working. Yes the university supplied jobs are that cushy.

After genuinely being friends with other smart and influential people and knowing them for a while, tell them you are looking for a better job/higher salary. Tell them what experience you have and talk about ideas you have about teaching, techniques you like. Then they will know that you are a passionate teacher. This will reduce the risk for them if they recommend you to a friend who has a job going. Don't be afraid to ask if they know of any opening positions or if they can introduce you to teaching opportunities.

Pros:

- The vast majority of jobs in Japan are known as 非公開 hikoukai - Not publicized. If you find a job through people, you will have little to no competition and much more room to negotiate your rate.
- The best positions often are 非公開 hikoukai - in terms of working conditions, benefits and potential for advancement.

Cons:

- You have to know someone to get these kinds of positions.
- If you do something wrong like show up late for the interview, or if after a few months you don't do as well as expected and are fired, your friend will likely hear about it. This may even damage their reputation a bit.

That can be devastating for some people but it is life. It is just a part of the working world because sometimes people just aren't right for a certain job or don't fit into that workplace's culture. Sometimes it comes down to circumstances, sometimes it comes down to who you work with. If this happens, the right thing to do is tell your friend who helped you get the position first so they hear it from you.

For you, networking is a simple case of being willing to put yourself out there, and also helping other people. For example, if you know someone who is looking for work and you know someone who is looking for a worker, and you can put those two people together, you have helped them out **and they will be willing to help you out in the future**. These will be people who know you and trust you because you have been a genuine help in their lives, and they will be happy to put themselves out there to recommend you for jobs that aren't even on the market.

The best jobs aren't on GaijinPot

As we said before, most of the best English teaching jobs in Japan are never even advertised as the most prestigious schools and academies already know a lot of the better teachers in the area through acquaintances or current staff, and they will use their expanded network to find those people rather than putting out an expensive ad or paying a recruiter to find someone. Know those people, meet them at events, through other friends, and by talking to people. Genuinely help them out and they will help you.

I know this one is harder to define and actively work on but there are tons of great opportunities out there if you have a good network of people who know that you are a passionate teacher.

Using Your Experience to get better English Teaching Jobs

Once you have been teaching in Japan for a while, and your interview skills are top notch, you can start to leverage this to get the higher paying jobs. This is the route that many teachers take. Usually, informal teaching experience alone doesn't open up all of the avenues to advance your career and make more money in Japan. I've met a lot of foreigners here who haven't gained any formal qualifications to teach English but ended up staying here, desperately trying to move up the corporate ladder at a big eikaiwa or dispatch company so they can support themselves or their family.

I was lucky to start working in Japan as a Peppy Kid's Club teacher. For all their faults, they had the most comprehensive new teacher training of any company I have ever worked for in Japan. They gave me two weeks of intensive training with practice demos on a daily basis, as well as teaching experience in schools, watching more experienced teachers do their lessons and lots and lots of feedback on my teaching style. When applying for other jobs I used a lot of the skills I learned from Peppy's training to show them that I was capable, and especially in being able to prepare a lesson and demo effectively.

A fellow Peppy teacher told me that after getting a teaching job at an English acting school in Tokyo, he was told that he got the job based on his incredible demo. While other people floundered, lacking experience in mock teaching scenarios, my friend was blowing the competition away and making the hiring manager's job very very easy. Demo skills can stand you in good stead for your entire career in Japan.

Job hopping

If you have some teaching experience, honed interview skills and a qualification to show off your academic skills, you can start job hopping and increasing your salary. Moving from job to job is not usually an option for Japanese people, but for foreigners it isn't so bad as most Japanese companies expect us to leave Japan after a year or two anyway. Those staying longer can reap the benefits of this stereotype. Heck even I thought I would only be in Japan for a year when I first got here!

Charlie Moritz shared a memory.
14 August at 22:24

He said, remaining in Japan for 4 more years and counting!

4 Years Ago
See your memories >

Charlie Moritz
14 August 2012

In 24 hours I'll be on a plane to Japan, not to return until September 2013!!!

👍 Like   💬 Comment   ↗ Share

Warning:

One thing you won't want to do for your reputation is to just quit a job mid-way through. **Loyalty is extremely important in Japan**, so jumping ship mid way through a contract and screwing over your company will likely hurt your future prospects, or at least raise questions. Be ready to answer them in a calm way that shows that you were just too good for that terrible job (which you are).

Job hopping gets you a better salary than staying at a company.

After a few years working at the same company, I thought back to how much money I made, how many hours I worked and what I had gained from repositioning myself to earn a higher monthly rate. I figured out what my hourly rate really was for my first five jobs in Japan, and it wasn't as nice as I thought.

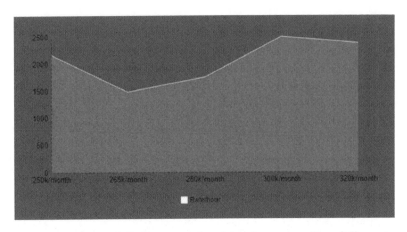

An increase in full time pay, but hourly rates tell a different story

My first job actually paid me better *per hour* than my next two jobs. Sure I was earning more at the other positions, and I learned more from working there than I ever could have sticking around at the first company, but I was putting way more time into work. Once you have some experience under your belt, it doesn't need to be this way.

Have you ever been in a situation where you have a job that pays really well and from the outside looks amazing, but was actually making you miserable? I was making nearly 4m yen a year working at a world famous kindergarten, but the work environment was horrible. The staff were always tense and worried about getting yelled at by the directors for not cleaning up properly, not standing right or not using the right pen when writing kids' birthday cards!

You think I'm joking? They once pulled me aside for a sit-down meeting with one of the directors because I was too close to the paper while I was writing (context: I'm near sighted).They told me that it was a bad image to present in front of the children that I was so close when writing and I should have better posture and that I needed to fix this "flaw".

I'd never before *wished that my school had been paying me less* so that I could have a good reason to go out and find another job. There was just no competition in terms of pay. The only way I could earn that much as an English teacher would have been a university job or an international school that needed teachers to have a teaching licence.

When it came time to renew my contract, I had already been looking around to set myself up for the next job using this strategy I had been wanting to try.

The strategy I'm about to tell you is risky. If you are the kind of person who will put up with awful work conditions to guarantee a certain salary, this is not for you. This strategy requires you to be resilient, capable and fantastic at interview, and generally be capable of performing the job and role of English teacher in many different situations to a high level. Being qualified was pretty critical for me and helped me get into a lot of interviews where I could show off my skills, but I've met people doing the same thing who have no special teaching qualifications. This is really hard to do if you don't have experience teaching (at least 2 or 3 years) and a great record.

The secret really is that...

Part-time work pays better than full-time work

If you can get enough part-time work, you can earn a lot more than you could at your full-time job.

Let me explain. I had been looking on JobsinJapan and

GaijinPot for part-time jobs and noticed that the hourly rate was sometimes double that of my supposedly high-paying job. I thought:

"Why the heck am I putting up with these awful work conditions and long days when I could just get two or three of these jobs, work half the hours and make just as much money?"

So I applied for **dozens** of them from January to April. I followed up my applications and made sure that I was gearing every application towards the specific position so I would get a lot of callbacks. I wrote cover letters for every single job position. I met with employers and hiring managers and did research on their companies and impressed them at the interview. This is a skill that you'll need to build if you want to find success as an English teacher, but also in life inside or outside of Japan.

A great mentor of mine in the UK once told me that when you are looking for a job, you should treat that as a full-time job. So when you are trying to change your work:

"Looking for a job <u>is</u> your job."

Be organised about it, get an excel spreadsheet with all the jobs you've applied to, the people to talk to and latest developments so you don't lose track. Get out there every day and *hustle*.

By May of 2016 I had 3 part-time jobs netting me ¥260k per month (until August), but instead of working 40 hours a week I was doing 18 (plus travel of about 6). I had Wednesdays and weekends completely off. For me this was about as freeing as I could have ever hoped for, and it only got better from there.

By summer of 2106 I had landed some sweet jobs paying me ¥10,000 per class four times per week (1 hour and 20 minutes) and a few others getting me ¥4000 and ¥5000 per hour. I had some months (September) where I made ¥420k while still only working 20 hours per week! This is the power of part-time work, and the lower responsibilities mean that for many of them, once you leave the school you don't have any homework or extra weekend responsibilities that you are roped into. If you value your free time (or like me need your free time to work on other projects) then mixing and matching part-time work is a great path to it.

If you only have one job, do you think that it is secure?

Even if they really like you, do you have personal and financial security. The answer always has to be no, right? At any time your boss can just tell you "we don't need you anymore, you're fired." Where is your security then? You can sue them but in Japan especially, it can be really hard to sue an employer, especially if you don't speak Japanese very well. Bilingual lawyers are expensive.

Furthermore, what do you have to do to try and maintain your position when you have that kind of axe looming over you? You have to suck up to the boss, of course. If they tell you that you have to work overtime, then you'll probably do it just to make sure they don't replace you. Believe me, foreigners are much more replaceable in Japan than you think! I've seen people just joining a company and getting fired **while in training**! That's definitely not security, and that girl ended up several thousand dollars out of pocket (for flights and accommodation) and jobless in a foreign country.

You can be like many other smart and driven foreigners in Japan. If you have a few jobs at any given time, when one of your bosses adds more and more to your workload and won't give you any more money for the overtime you're working, or your working conditions at one job are terrible and you hate the people, you can quit and you'll still have enough coming in to pay your bills.

When you have a few streams of income you can decide what work you want to prioritise and what work you want to drop. There are always part-time jobs going on the jobs boards, through friends or through applying via the direct method we talked about earlier in this chapter. Recently these are less common on GaijinPot because their ad prices are too high for part-time positions, but there are lots of better places to find them now.

When You Go For Part-time Jobs In Japan, Start To Think Of Your Salary By Year.

I'm not going to lie, some months I got some frankly embarrassing paychecks. In July a lot of the schools had summer break so my pay for that month was only ¥180k. However, once you do your taxes for the whole year you'll see what the difference is. For me it was only working about 15-20 hours per week on four days, and still beating my previous year's salary by more than ¥400k. I also got a massive tax refund of ¥285k from overpaying tax through my various different jobs.

At the same time I've had enough time working from home to build **Live Work Play Japan** and start freelancing as a web developer, doing yoga in the mornings, reading books, going on trips to explore Japan and just generally having more time to do the stuff I wanted to do when I came here in the first place.

If you're at all like me and feel like you've had enough making an artificially capped English teacher salary and want to learn new skills, get better at what you do and make more free time for yourself, you might want to try getting some part-time jobs on the side. Working much harder for more money is rarely the way to go for expats in Japan, and you can make more money with less time investment if you apply what we've been talking about here.

I don't care if I make 20% more money if I have to work 40% more.

I wasn't just looking on job boards (though at first that was a big part of the reason I was able to make it as a part-timer). Once you've had a few jobs and met other interesting foreigners who are gaming the system too, you can start using the strategies we talked about like using your network and the trusty Grandpa Method.

For me, part-time work was a way out of the nine-to-five (or eight-to-six-thirty in some of my jobs in Japan). Finding the right jobs and being able to work effectively there, avoiding the landmines that we have talked about in this guide, will help you have more security and better pay for less and less of your time.

Become a Teachapreneur

Get a side hustle going and potentially earn more than you could in a regular job by private tutoring as a freelance teacher.

Already we have explored some of your options for increasing your salary by job hopping. We also discussed the Grandpa Method and Direct methods where you go directly to employers for work the old fashioned way. We also talked about the Savvy Teacher method in which you utilize your network to get recommendations for opportunities you would have never found elsewhere. Remember too that we discussed 非公開求人案件 *Hikoukai Kyujin Anken* "Secret job listings" that you cannot find on any public site such as Jobs in Japan or GaijinPot.

Put all that together and clearly the most effective way to increase your exposure to the teaching market is to put in place a versatile strategy of attack. Let everyone in your network know you are an aspiring teacher and when you see potential opportunities, ask someone. While your friends may not always know of immediate job opportunities, they can introduce you to Japanese who are often seeking out English tutoring.

Once you've met one mom who wants you to tutor her son, as long as you are open and approachable, she will likely introduce you to more moms. You can choose to specialize in adults, teens or children. You can be as selective or open as you choose. At first, just like job hunting it can be hard to find people willing to pay you for English lessons. You may not feel comfortable at first asking for due compensation. Over time, you will better understand how to approach people for tutoring opportunities. You will learn how to teach one on one as opposed to teaching larger lecture and more importantly, how much one hour of time with you is really worth (hint, more than you likely think).

My Sensei.com and iTalki

Sites like my-sensei.com, italki.com, and even regular social media sites like Facebook can be great places to start looking for students. Martin made a profile on My Sensei while he taught at a private international school and quickly found students to privately teach.

Just like looking for jobs online anywhere, competition is pretty fierce. You are now selling your services to customers instead of businesses or schools when you are offering lessons on these sites. It is similar to selling on eBay. You gain more access to potential buyers through eBay, but you have drawbacks. There can be a race to the bottom (everybody trying to be the cheapest) if you are offering the same type of English teaching services as others on the site. It helps to differentiate yourself by offering unique lesson structures, working on your personal brand marketing (good photos, testimonials etc.) and spending a little time hustling. The other way in which is like selling on eBay is that My Sensei can become your new and very strict boss. If someone leaves you a poor review, if you forget to cancel a lesson on the site or even something as innocent as yawn during your lesson, your listing can be penalized or possibly even removed.

Some of the best rates can be found doing business tutoring, and Charlie regularly has business dinners with small groups of international sales teams in an import/export company and gets paid ¥10,000 (plus dinner) to talk and be interested in international business (an easy thing to be interested in).

The nice thing about private tutoring as well is that you can set you own hours and have as many or as few responsibilities as you care to take on. Here all you need to do is convince someone to pay you for English classes, and if you only want to have one hour per week on top of your other job(s), there's nothing wrong with that. When you accept a full time job, you are all in. You can't work two full time teaching gigs. You can tutor students on the side for an hour or two per week. Over time, you will become better at teaching, your reputation will improve and you can earn more from private students. You can even turn this into your full time business if you're good enough, like Charlie's friend Julian from the UK who expanded his business English teaching to start his own company.

Think of sites like My Sensei as a way to get started tutoring. The Savvy Teacher method will get you much further. Ultimately, word of mouth is the most effective way to gain access to more students and better paying students. If you teach at a K-12 school, you may find opportunities to privately tutor your students through their parents, and moms love to talk about their kid's favorite English teacher.

Get In the Way of Opportunities

Advice from Diego for becoming an indispensable teacher:

My personal strategy, and one that has repeatedly reaped great rewards over the years, is to be a big fish in a little pond. Since the 1980s, thousands of young Western men and women have flocked to Japan to teach English. After the bubble burst in the 1990s, people continued to come despite the stagnant economy and declining wages. After more than two decades of stilted economic growth and an ever increasing number of foreign workers, new teachers find themselves in a difficult situation. Starting wages are relatively low, work conditions are not especially good, social respect for the kind of work you do is low, and there is someone who wants to replace you around every corner. Unless you have specialized skills, you are expendable to most companies.

Being a big fish in a little pond means you should find your market niche and chase it. Specialize in a particular subject area or skill and become the go-to person for it. If you build your resume with a specialization in either debate, speech, technology, politics, the natural sciences, drama, dance, hospitality, or cross-cultural communication, for example, you position yourself to be the first person thought of when a position in that field opens up. The teaching community is small, especially in higher education. Your reputation will open doors, and you can use that to scaffold your way up the food chain.

When I came to Japan, I had a master's degree in international affairs and work experience in politics and government. I knew I didn't want to teach English for the long term, at least not directly, so I made it a point to pursue as many political/governmental/social studies related opportunities as possible.

One of these positions came from a Craigslist ad asking for judges to observe a student debate. The ad was low on details, somewhat sketchy, and advertised an unpaid position, but in the realm of my political experience and would put me in a new and challenging position. I emailed my resume and offered my time, but I soon received a reply letting me know there were no remaining availabilities. I forgot about it until a few months later I received an email asking me to come in for some kind of interview. The organization had begun a new program partnering with senior high schools in the city to teach a year-long debate course. I accepted and spent a year at a girls school building teaching credibility at a decent wage.

I didn't stop there - I used all my agency to shape the direction of those debate classes. I geared them toward government and international politics, allowing me to add those important lines to my resume. I was able to do that because I took control of the classroom and because they are topics I am personally interested in and passionate about.

During this time, I was also teaching English at a senior high school where I was able to design the curriculum. I made sure to create several units that examined world politics, economics, and governance, using authentic documents and case studies to be able to continue the political/governmental theme in my resume.

During the summer I found an organization that held empowerment programs for high school students by having them discuss real-world issues, like global warming and conflict. I leveraged the experiences I'd already amassed to secure this job. I worked all summer and in the fall began to target social studies related teaching positions.

The following school year, I was hired to teach social studies (international relations and political science) at a prestigious high school, and accepted an offer to teach one of the few international studies courses at a well-regarded university, based largely on the fact that my resume was one of the very few in Tokyo to mention building analytical thinking skills and argumentative abilities, discussing topics like globalization, global warming, and democratic governance. I'd become a big fish in a little pond, and my presence was impossible to ignore.

Be So Good They Can't Ignore You

The point is that you should do your best to accept any opportunity you come across in your chosen field, either paid or not, either at the educational level you desire to work in or not, whether you feel like it or not. It's impossible to see where all the links these jobs create might go to in the future, but if you create a profile of indispensable skills, held only by a small group of people, you become much more valuable.

Japan is littered with 20-somethings that have a couple of years of eikaiwa or ALT work under their belts, many of whom are looking to make more money and are all competing against you. Without specialization, the only way to win that game is luck, and that's something you should never rely on. Think of yourself, and by extension your resume, and all the experiences and projects you've worked on, the conferences you've attended and presented at, and even the clubs and organizations you join in your personal time, as a brand. What is your brand? How strong is it? Would a reputable university buy it? As long as your answers are maybe or no, you have more work to do.

Thanks to the increasing popularity of a method of teaching called Content and Language Integrated Learning (CLIL), and the growing number of foreign students enrolled in all-English university programs, English teaching is no longer the only path available if you're seeking a university job. Depending on your qualifications, and your brand, there are opportunities to teach nearly any subject at the university level.

Do you have a technology background, perhaps a bachelor's in computer science or a certificate in I.T.? Look on Craigslist or on school websites or any of the several job sites for volunteer or low-pay positions teaching kids to program, or (depending on your Japanese ability) stop by your city office and see if they have any technology tutoring programs in the community center. Browse Ohayo Sensei for a computer science summer camp (I've seen them), or check GaijinPot for week-long business English seminars at tech firms. If all else fails, offer private English lessons based around technology. Distribute fliers outside major technology firms at a discounted price. Remember, the goal right now is not to make money, it's to build your brand. You'll only need to get one student before you can advertise yourself as an experienced technology educator. Think of your career as a ladder, and your goal is to get up to the next step. The higher you go, the easier it will be to use your previous experience to create your next opportunity.

If you're following a more traditional path and are pursuing TESOL or other forms of English teaching a the university level, take some time and review the qualifications listed on university job listings (websites where these jobs are posted are listed in the Tools and Resources section). You will find a fair number that ask with a familiarity with American or British literature, or with specific experience in business/financial English, or academic English. Decide which you'd like to pursue and plot your course according to your goals. Even if you have a degree in American literature, if all your experience is in teaching babies the days of the week, you're not going to get very far. If you can't find a position, make one, begin a book club and advertise it on meetup.com. It may seem low effort to you, but you'd be surprised how few people will take that extra step to stand out.

Teaching at University in Japan: Freedom, Career Growth and Top Industry Pay

Diego Medrano has built an incredible career for himself in Japan by building a reputation that lets him teach at some of the most famous and prestigious universities in Japan. Aside from making an incredible living, past what any ALT or eikaiwa teacher could dream of, he also loves the work and gets to teach what he is passionate about rather than just canned English lessons. This is advanced stuff, but remember that you can always come back to this book and reread this section when you have the experience or qualifications you need to branch out into university teaching.

Why Teach at University

The only way you're going to be successful at going down this path, at making a successful career out of teaching and being a university educator, is by really believing in the power that a teacher can have in the lives of their students. I live by the belief that teaching is not a job, it's a vocation. When I put on my tie and pick up my briefcase, when I swipe a stick of chalk against the smooth blackboard, and when I grade my students' assignments and exams, I'm inhabiting a role in society.

Being an educator is an incredible thing: on our best days, we can help our students see the world in an entirely new light, exposing them to complex and fascinating ideas. Watching my students grow and mature is entirely satisfying, professionally and personally, and leaves me with a sense of worth in what I do. On our worst days, we're the reason young men and women get rejected from the best graduate schools for their programs, or the job of their dreams. Being a teacher is an awesome responsibility, and you must remember that fact and respect it. In exchange for all of that, you will be at the top of your earning potential as an educator in Japan.

University compared to eikaiwa and public school teaching

*Full-time eikaiwa teachers hustle to try and break ¥3 million per year. Full-time university positions pay **at least double** that.*

*Full-time eikaiwa teachers may have up to 40 teaching hours per week. Full-time university positions range from **10-20 teaching hours** per week.*

*Eikaiwa teachers get extremely limited time off, often not being able to take vacations until at least six months after joining, sometimes only in their second year, and even then only 10 days per year are paid. University teachers get between 1-3 months off per year, **fully paid**.*

*Eikaiwa teachers are commodities, replaceable, typically powerless, and are forced to teach whatever material their company gives them. University teachers are much more difficult to replace, they often have **influence** within their department, and **autonomy to create the kind of lessons they want**.*

The list could go on and on.

The market is competitive, but there are steps you can take to greatly increase your chances of landing a university teaching position. I'll share my own setup, which resulted in four university job offers last hiring season, three of which offered competitive salaries and three months of paid vacation. This was done without a professional university-level network, or even prior university teaching experience.

How can I teach at a university in Japan?

The most common question I'm asked concerning university teaching is whether or not you can get a university job without a graduate degree. My answer is always the same: **No.**

Of course there are exceptions to the rule: the friend who was in the right place at the right time, the acquaintance who went far enough into the countryside they found a university willing to hire them, or the disillusioned expat sitting at the bar gobbling down every free peanut they can as they work the university dispatch circuit. The fact is, high quality, high paying jobs require high quality candidates. For universities who have a reputation and responsibilities to their students, this means advanced degrees.

If you do not have a master's degree already, do not let this discourage you. It is possible to earn a master's degree while living and working in Japan, typically within two years. If you believe Japan will be your home for the foreseeable future, and you have decided to make a career out of teaching, a two year commitment is a small price to pay.

The Japan Student Services Organization is an excellent source for finding graduate programs throughout the country that are offered in English (check the resources section for a link). Consider the field you would like to teach in and review the degree programs available to you. One thing you should consider: while universities are actively growing their English-based curriculums and offering a greater diversity of classes in English, the majority of university teaching positions will be in TESOL. Of course - especially with the growing popularity of CLIL - it is possible to find jobs teaching in almost any field in Japan, however the more niche or specialized the subject, the more difficult it will be finding work teaching it, and the more likely it will be for you to need a doctorate or being highly distinguished in your field. Temper your intellectual passions with the realities of the job market.

In addition to traditional education, I have colleagues who received their master's degrees through distance learning programs. I can't speak to how these degrees are viewed or valued in the workplace, however, I've met successful university lecturers who attained their degree in this way (at a substantial discount compared to the cost of a traditional school).

A quick note about the cost of attending a university in Japan: prices are generally around ¥800,000 per year, depending on the program. While this is not cheap, it is far less expensive than attending a graduate school in the United States. You must also keep in mind your future earning potential. Don't balk at a short-term cost when the long-term benefits greatly exceed it.

Keep in mind that simply having a master's degree does not guarantee that you will find work. You'll need to build your teaching experience and try to become published while in school to become competitive. Many teachers will spend a year or two teaching senior high school to build this kind of experience, some find that they like it so much, they stay.

Where and when to find University positions

The best university jobs never make it to a public listing, and often the ones that do are made with someone already in mind. Start building your network and your profile and you will find your job that way. Build your network by being around other teachers, either at conferences, seminars, universities, or job interviews. Join a few of the many teaching organizations in Japan (you can find a list in the Resources section): each one should have large conferences or seminars or even training sessions. Show up and collect business cards. You will often meet university teachers doing odd jobs to make ends meet - ask them to get a beer or grab dinner. When the department head asks them to find a new teacher for the spring semester, your name might spring to mind.

Failing that, jREC-IN and JALT are two of the most active websites for university teaching jobs in Japan. Many universities, however, will still post new positions directly onto their homepage, so it's a good idea to check there as well. Some positions are advertised through Ohayo Sensei, though that is becoming rarer and these positions typically pay lower salaries.

The Hiring Seasons in Japan

The school year begins in April and ends in February. Most major universities have two hiring seasons: the first and biggest season is from October-December. Some positions will open earlier, but the majority will appear around November/December. This is when schools are deciding who to invite back, who to promote, and who to let go. The second hiring season is in February/March.

This is when schools are scrambling to fill up any last minute positions they couldn't find a qualified candidate for, or just found out that someone who agreed to teach is now withdrawing. I know someone who was hired by his university on April 3rd, and their first day of class was on April 7th. While rare, these positions do exist and can be a good chance for a less qualified/experienced teach to get their foot into the door.

One somewhat controversial method of applying for jobs in the blind scattershot. Basically, this entails putting your resume into a bunch of enveloped and sending them to every school you can think of. It's a time-consuming and costly method, perhaps not a smart thing to do when you are over-worked and poor. I don't believe it should be totally disregarded, however, because I used it my first year in Tokyo and it got me a job offer. I ultimately turned the offer down, but it was a good job for a good salary (summer pay included). I had sent fifty envelopes stuffed with a cover letter, my resume, and a letter of recommendation for that one offer. I saved a lot of time by make a spreadsheet with the schools' names, addresses, and contact persons, then using autofill in Microsoft Word to customize each letter. Nobody likes to receive an unsolicited letter, so I phrased my cover letter as if I was replying to a job announcement. At least if some of these schools were actively recruiting, they would think I was just another applicant. It was a crapshoot, but it did have some success.

As stated before, try not to count on luck to get you a job. Make yourself and your specializations well known and jobs will come to you. I've had two job offers that I ultimately accepted come to me through distant acquaintances, simply because they associated me with the kind of job that was being offered. Any time someone I knows seeing something political or governmental or social studies-y, I get a message. When your profile becomes big enough, you won't need to actively search for work, the work will come to you.

Salary Information

Part-Time Lecturers: Work less and earn a full-time salary

Universities will typically pay **by the koma**, that is, by the class. It doesn't matter how many times you meet that month or how many hours long it is, you'll receive a flat rate each month. Salary per koma for a beginning university position is typically around ¥28,000-¥30,000 per month. This means that if you teach three classes per day, five days per week, you'll receive approximately ¥425,000 per month. This kind of schedule can be difficult to put together, however, since most schools only offer two day combinations (Tuesday and Friday or Monday and Thursday). You will often find university lecturers that teach university four days a week and then do something different on that extra day to make extra income.

Classes are 90 minutes long, and the majority of universities begin first period around 09:00. Third period ends around 15:00. If you aren't use to 24 hour time, get use to it - most schools use it for all official documents. Graduate classes will typically meet later in the evening.

You'll have two months off with pay in the summer (July-September), and one month off with pay in the winter (March). You will not have a private office, but you will likely have a desk in some kind of communal teacher's room. There are few benefits, but likewise, there are few responsibilities outside of class. Your transportation will be fully reimbursed and you should have access to university resources, like the library, research assistance, and journal access.

Full-Time Lecturers

You will receive a flat rate, whatever the overtime or number of classes you teach. Salaries range greatly, but typically a full-time teacher will begin between ¥5 to ¥6 million per year. Some universities tend to be conservative in the way they are run, and as such you may encounter instances will salary is determined not by your total experience or ability, but on your age. This can be frustrating and seem unfair, however, as you will discover often is the case in Japan, there is often no way around it. At other universities, salary increases according to experience. If you were making ¥3 million a year at your previous position and are not making double, you'll have paid for your ¥1.6 million master's degree within the first year.

I should note, however, that it is becoming increasingly difficult to find a full-time position at a university, even if you are not tenured. For a lot of reasons, Japanese universities have spent the last two decades moving toward the part-time model. While there are definitely full-time positions available, there are more competitive and will generally require a PhD and several years of experience.

As full-time staff, you should be receiving additional benefits from the university, including a pension, special health care coverage, perhaps a housing allowance, perhaps a research allowance, access to research grants, sponsorship to attend conferences, and a few other perks. You will generally be expected to work all year long, attending office meetings and keeping office hours even when school is not in session, though some schools are very lenient during summer and winter break. Tenure is a possibility but not a guarantee, and you will be expected to publish and do some curriculum development.

Tenured Professors

At this level having a PhD is a minimum requirement. You will likely need to have a number of publications, conference presentations, and some kind of distinguishing accomplishment. You are not simply an instructor in your field, but a leader in your field. You'll write the books your students read.

A tenured professor's salary can range, depending on field and qualification. I've known professors with salaries of ¥10 million, and professors with salaries of ¥7 million. Just as with your master's, you can earn your PhD in an all-English program while living in Japan. This is one of the hardest positions to attain in Japan, but once you get there it can be one of the cushiest, highest-paying jobs you'll ever get. Well worth working towards if you have long term plans to further your teaching career in Japan.

Teaching is a valuable skill for the long-term

We know that people don't always stick in English teaching for the long term. Hey, even Charlie gets most of his work freelancing as a web developer in Tokyo now. However, the skills you learn as an English teacher can help you not only to move up the ladder, but also give you a lot of experience with **soft skills** that will set you up for success in Japan and back home.

The pathways up are always there, and if you take the time to get the qualifications and get an English teaching position at a university in Japan, you'll have a very cushy job as we talked about earlier. Great pay, months of the year off and paid travel for conferences; teaching at university is a golden opportunity for people with the right qualifications.

But even if you decide to get out of English teaching, the strategies we're talking about will help you in your future career. A lot of the soft skills of English teaching apply to jobs in every industry:

- Working in a team and with others (team-teaching, working with multicultural teams and communicating across language barriers).
- Writing an effective CV/resume and cover letter, and techniques to land a job that set you out from the crowd.
- Networking skills and connecting with people in a meaningful way.

We wrote this guide to help you with the skills and cultural knowledge that we have gained over years of living in Japan and performing at the highest levels of our industries. The journey is where the real learning happens. That is where you distinguish yourself as a top performer and not just another "holiday English teacher" looking to help pay for an extended vacation in Japan.

Do you need to speak Japanese?

We have already mentioned many times in the book already and on our blog how learning Japanese can be a huge differentiator for you. Pretty much, every aspect of Japanese life gets better if you speak Japanese. Let's not pretend that it doesn't. That all being said, do you need to speak Japanese to get in the top percentile of English teachers in Japan, both in terms of pay and status? No. You can get there without speaking much at all.

This is because many of the paths to leveling up as an English teacher end in teaching at a high paying international school or university. That is what we focus on in this book, but by no means do we think that you ought to stick it out in education if it isn't right for you. If you have other skills, Japanese included, you could go from English teacher to a well-compensated market team researcher for Uniqlo, Rakuten or Shinsei bank.

We always recommend that you put some serious effort into learning Japanese. Even if you don't need it to get an amazing job, it will always be beneficial to you in Japan. If you studied Japanese for twenty minutes every lunch break for three years, there is no universe in which you shouldn't be a fluent speaker of Japanese. Another few years and you'd be reading newspapers. By that time, you could be an entrepreneur, a business owner or manager, living somewhere you never imagined you could. Keep up your pursuits of self-improvement in your job life and keep learning Japanese.

Is Japanese Useful After I Leave Japan?

Are you worried that after five years of teaching English in Japan you will be unemployable when you return to your home country?

Nonsense. You got five years of intense international communications studies under your belt now. You learned to adapt to a culture completely different than your own and now you know how to negotiate with Japanese. Even if you didn't learn Japanese to business level by this point, you know how to talk to Japanese better than anyone else in your home town. You know the faces they make when they are upset, you know what their body language means, and you know what they like to do. That, plus drive, is all you would need in an international company working with the Japanese market.

What if you did what I suggested above and just studied Japanese for twenty minutes a day every lunch break for those six years? Well, you can now get a bilingual job with hundreds of Japanese company branches and head offices all around the globe. Toyota Tsusho, Honda, Astellas. These are just some of the many Japanese companies that employ American citizens in the US. They are always looking for bilinguals who can better communicate with their customer base and their related branches back in Japan. Even a JLPT level 3 student will fair a chance at a bilingual job back in their home country. If you follow my simple twenty minutes at lunch plan and study progressively more challenging materials, you should have no problem with at least the JLPT level 2.

Is Japanese necessary to get high paying jobs in Japan?

I'm sure you have read on forums, Facebook groups and reddit that the only way to get a better job in Japan is to learn to speak business level Japanese. This is far from the truth, and there are hundreds of foreigners that I know in Japan who are not great speakers of Japanese but have awesome, high-paying jobs.

Really, your skill and proven track record are the strongest indicators to prospective employers that they should hire you. If you're a great English teacher, it won't *always* bother them so much that you don't speak Japanese. Having said that, at least conversational Japanese ability is a huge bonus to your chances of success both on your resume and at interview, as well as within any company you are working for. Speaking Japanese, at least a little bit, shows Japanese hiring managers that you are willing to engage with their culture. There is nothing that turns a school off working with foreigners more than someone who won't engage with Japanese customs. Having a teacher who can speak some Japanese lets the school relax a little bit. They won't have to worry that you will be wandering around not knowing what to do because you didn't even try to understand the announcement over the speaker system.

On one occasion, Charlie was actually called in to the office to help the headmaster interpret over Skype. They would be giving a speech at a school in China the following month and needed someone to help interpret. The Chinese lady on the other end of the call could speak English, but Charlie's school's headmaster couldn't speak much at all. The interpreters at the school were busy with parent-teacher meetings, and there was nobody else to help with the skype conversation. Even with just a conversational level in Japanese, Charlie was able to convey the basic information and get it across to both parties, which gave him a lot of good will with the school who were very happy that he could step up to help them.

Another common scenario is working with Japanese teachers (usually in ALT positions, who don't understand much English. If you listen to the give-up gaijin, you might think that it is insane that a Japanese teacher of English could hardly speak a word of English. Satou-sensei might have actually been a math teacher in elementary schools for years.He switches school and perhaps that school doesn't have enough English teachers, but has plenty of math teachers. The school board needs him to teach English. Did he major in English in school? No. Has he even studied English since college? No. Satou sensei now has to teach a subject he does not know well. He will rely on the textbook and test prep almost entirely. That is the whole purpose of hiring a gaikokujin to be an ALT.

The school board knows Sato-sensei is not good at speaking English. They would rather hire you if you can speak in Japanese because you can communicate with Satou sensei about lesson plans, games and whatever else you want to do in class. If you don't already speak Japanese, this is the perfect chance for you to learn.

There is no excuse to not learn Japanese unless you actually have current and set in stone plans to leave Japan very soon. Even if you believe that you'll only be in Japan for a short while, spending the time learning a new, valuable skill like Japanese is a no-brainer. You never know when you might decide that Japan is your home for the foreseeable future. Why not give it a go?

How can I learn Japanese?

Just learning Japanese can separate you from thousands of other gaikokujin in Japan competing with you for jobs. As an added plus, it's just plain cool! I have spoken Spanish for years, but never did people turn their heads to see me speaking Spanish. Japanese and Mandarin though? People will notice that. Employers notice as well. If you haven't yet, take a look at the article on Live Work Play Japan where I make the case for Japanese as a major advantage even for those looking for jobs in the Americas and Europe.

If I could start learning Japanese again from scratch, what would he do?

I would go with an audio focused course with lots of listening input. Reading and writing is cool, and very useful, but the first skills that people learn in their native language are listening, speaking, then reading and finally writing, right? Take an audio course like this one from JapanesePod101 and you'll have a massive head-start on people who are trying to memorize word lists from a textbook.

Japanesepod101.com – Learn Japanese with Free Daily Podcasts

For more advanced language learners who want to use the best techniques to get fluent in Japanese fast, take a look Glossika, possibly the best language learning audio course out there. Glossika was developed by a guy named Michael Campbell, who is well known for his mastery of Mandarin and Chinese dialects like Taiwanese.

Glossika's program introduces you to thousands of unique whole sentences in spaced repetition sequences. You only are exposed to words in context, as you would in your native language. You learn these sentences by hearing their translation, copying and repeating (as babies do) and reading it in the ebooks. As you learn these, you are picking up the rhythm of the language and intonation.

Glossika

Learn Japanese Fast with Glossika

The first skill in any language to focus on is: Listening

You will be working on this skill forever, as you do in your native tongue. It's where babies start. I believe that if you cannot hear certain sounds, you truly cannot make them. Many Japanese admit to not being able to hear the difference between L and R, thus their "lows" are sometimes "rows" and visa-versa.

Actually this is a good thing to know, especially if you are an English teacher, but also as a language learner. Ironically, many English speakers struggle with the Japanese "R" as in 楽天 *Rakuten*. The English "ra" is just different from the Japanese ら sound.

If you cannot do a soft roll of your Rs, just use L. Every time you see a word with the hirigana らりるれろ ra ri ru re ro, just pretend they are "Ls" and everyone in Japan will understand you perfectly. The better your listening gets, the better your pronunciation will become, the more fluent you will become.

Fluency is the most important goal of language. Professor Paul Nation is famous for his language learning research and teacher training programs. He insists that the goal of every language learning activity no matter what the skill (listening, speaking, reading, writing) being trained should be fluency. Listen fluently, speak fluently, read fluently and write fluently. Even if you are just learning 10 words, the target is fluency in use of those 10 words. Once you are fluent at 10 words, it is much easier to keep the fluency going. It is hard to become fluent after you have learned hundreds and thousands of words.

I take this to heart with every language I learn. When I am reading a passage in Japanese, you may think my only goal is to understand it. My goal is actually to read it fluently with a fluent understanding. I will re-read the same passage over and over again, sometimes even hand transcribe it if I need to, until I can read it quickly with accuracy and with understanding.

The Key is Consistency

Whatever you decide to do for learning Japanese, whether it be to pick up JapanesePod101, Genki or learn from a tutor, do that consistently. If you say "I am going to study Japanese for thirty minutes a day five days a week", do that. Don't stop for 3 days, then try to cram it all in on Friday and then forget to start back up on your regular schedule the following Monday. **Just like job hunting, most people do stuff for a while, stop, do other stuff, stop, do nothing and then wonder why they aren't getting results.** They question the method, the teacher, their own intelligence, anything they can to try to explain why they aren't getting the results they want. 99% of the time, it really is just because they aren't doing whatever they should do consistently. If something you are doing consistently with intent still doesn't get you to your goal, then and only then do you change your approach.

Set tangible, achievable goals

Have a set goal with a set date. Whatever you do to learn Japanese has to be done in agreement with your goal timeline. Think of ships leaving a harbor. One ship has no captain or crew. The sail opens. It would be a miracle if the ship even gets out of the harbor without wrecking. The second ship has a captain and crew but no set course. It leaves the harbor with no problem. Some months later it is found shipwrecked. The third ship not only has a captain and crew, but half of a map. Not even a whole map. This map shows how to start the journey and get the ship to wealthy trading port. This third ship not only successfully exits the harbor but it gets to the wealthy trading port. From there, it can refuel, trade goods and do reconnaissance on the ultimate destination.

The point is, it has a plan and even though the plan is not complete, the ship knows where it needs to go. From there, it is up to the captain to decide whether it is worth it or not to make a new plan to go to the ultimate destination.

That is a lot of what it's like learning new languages, especially Japanese. There are walls in Japanese you wouldn't even imagine no matter how many languages you can already speak. There is a reason they say that Japanese is the hardest language for native English speakers to learn. You must decide as the captain of your ship whether you are willing to make the journey. Don't start it half assed and shipwreck on a sandbar. At least get somewhere and make a choice of where to set sail.

Aim 1: Transactional Fluency

I would suggest aiming for what I call transactional fluency. This means you can communicate your basic needs for daily life fluently. From "Where is the bathroom?" and "Does this train go to such and such station?" to "I would like a large please." As a general rule, your ability to grasp input will be several times greater than your output ability. Once you can also understand the main transactional requests and demands people make to you in real time, we can say you are transactionally fluent. You probably cannot read more than 20% of a newspaper article if at all, but that is not your purpose at this point. You just want to become functional in Japan.

The JLPT: A Clear Path to Advanced Japanese

After your ship gets to the first wealthy port, you can make the decision to set sail for the ultimate destination. We talk a lot about Japanese on Live Work Play Japan because it is a really important part of learning to live in this beautiful country. The JLPT is a test that gives you proof of your skills, so if you are looking to get out of the English teaching game and spread your wings in Japan, learning the language to N2 or N1 level is one way to do that, though by no means the only way.

That isn't the top of the mountain by any means. I did pass that test finally some years ago. I can tell you that I already was working in a Japanese company before I passed, so not having the N1 doesn't mean you can't work in a Japanese company. Even once I had it, I could still open a regular book and find kanji I didn't recognize and words I didn't know. Learning Japanese is a lifelong pursuit, and after you become advanced you get to study the really fun stuff. If you are committed to passing the N1, the best advice I can give you is to set weekly targets to read real Japanese written content for Japanese by Japanese: books, 文庫 *bunko* small books, magazines, newspapers. Don't assume that living in Japan or studying from some kanji app on your phone will get you there. Read enough content in Japanese that you are interested in will show you kanji that you will come to know by second nature. Then passing the N1 will be easy for you, as it likely would be for a Japanese person.

Language Exchanges

Whether in Tokyo or a mountain town up north in Yamagata, we encourage you to go out to learn Japanese. Don't just stay home with your Genki textbook, as this is the number one way to make you hate learning Japanese and give up early. Go to language exchanges or events where you can meet native Japanese speakers. Meetup.com is by far the best for this in Japan, and not only for English speakers but also German, Chinese or Spanish too. Many lifelong friendships have been formed just from language exchanges, and Charlie met his girlfriend and some of his best friends at the language exchange meetup he started in Nagoya. If you meet people you like at these groups (not just for dating), do a language exchange with them over coffee. Set some parameters such as speaking in English for 30 minutes, then Japanese for 30. If your Japanese is just not to that level yet, you can simply ask your partner to help you through your textbook. Genki, Yookoso, Minna No Nihongo and other Japanese textbooks all have dialogues and speaking sections that you can practice with a partner if you like.

Remember that listening and speaking should be the focus until you have attained a confident level, then you can start on Kanji. All of the resources we have used to learn Japanese are on this book's page on our site at **liveworkplayjapan.com/teach-english**.

We felt it was important to discuss learning Japanese in this book, but if you have tried dozens of times and still can't get it, don't stress about it. There are plenty of foreigners living in Japan for a long time who don't speak Japanese, and while you may find some limits without confidence in Japanese, there are still more opportunities here than you can imagine for a foreigner with real skills to offer.

The Next Steps

As we near the end of this book, we wanted to remind you of the incredible opportunities for expats in Japan. We wrote this book to help those of you who love Japan and want to continue living, working and having fun here, but don't want to put up with the low rates that many English teachers just accept and try not to think about. A lot of them go back home no better off financially than when they first came to Japan, and sometimes even feeling bitter about the time they feel like they wasted here. A lot of them go back to a tough market where many people tell them that their time in Japan "doesn't look good" on their resume, and looks like a gap year from real life.

In this way there are two kinds of people who live in Japan: those who think that they control their own destiny and those who think others have control over their destiny. Just go on reddit or look in the Facebook groups about Japan (or better yet, don't); there are all manner of trolls there who will tell you that you can't do it. They will tell you that living in Japan will make you unhireable back home, or that they tried to get out of the low pay brackets but that Japan wouldn't let them. These people are to be avoided like the plague.

You absolutely can do whatever you want to do in Japan. As a non-Japanese you actually have a huge advantage in Japan of not having to conform to the ridiculous working hours that Japanese people are often pushed to give. The first limitation is yourself and your attitude. It can be said that a bad attitude is the worst thing you can have in Japan, and I was lucky that early on one of my close friends noticed that my defensive attitude was damaging my career in Japan, and that my habit of blaming others for all of my problems was going to keep me at the bottom of the ladder.

When you take responsibility for your own success in Japan, you get back in the driver's seat and you can control where you go.

You have awful co-workers? You're in control, and you have the choice to not let them ruin your life.

You didn't get that team leader job that would have bumped up your salary? Behave like a leader anyway, and if they don't see your value, find somewhere that does.

You got fired from your job for some weird cultural reason that makes no sense? *Fight for it or go out and find another job that will make you happy.*

That is the real message of this book: that you have the power to control your destiny in Japan, and you can control it if you are willing to learn how.

Read below to a header that describes where you are in your Japan journey now, and see what you can do next to get to Japan and maximise your potential income.

I don't live in Japan yet, how do I get to Japan?

The first thing you need to do is go to the Embassy for Japan in your home country to find out what your Visa requirements are. For some countries it is very hard to get a visa, so you'll want to know that before you go out there looking for a job as you might waste a lot of time. When you go to the embassy, talk to more than one person on more than one occasion if you can as they won't always look up the information to help you on your way. Keep a record of **who you talked to** and what they said, as nobody will follow up your requests if you just said "somebody at the embassy told me to do this."

They can offer you visa support and help you find out what you need to get a job teaching English in Japan. If you want to work, it can be hard only using the internet from your home country. The best way would be to visit Japan for at least a week or two and look directly here. Better, study Japanese here and you will have more time to look while you study. Hiring without an in-person interview is still uncommon in Japan. Also, speaking even a little Japanese will increase your prospects exponentially.

Read our section about getting your first job in Japan to actually start looking for and landing a job here.

I just moved to Japan, what now?

Your first task is to catalogue as many open positions you can find with English teaching companies, schools and agencies in your target area(s) in Japan and file this information into a list. Finding job opportunities is easier than ever thanks to online job boards, which is the easiest resource for new teachers to start building the experience and understanding you need to launch yourself into better paying jobs.

Then, you need to take action to line up interviews. You want as many decision makers in companies on your job list to see your resume as possible. Sticking with a school that sponsored your visa is only advisable if you really like the work you are doing and you're getting paid very well, as the overwhelming majority of schools won't scale your income with loyalty and years spent working there.

The key is to take action as quickly as possible. Don't get bogged down in research early on, as you'll mostly be looking for something further up the ladder, teaching an age group you feel comfortable with and can develop more understanding and ability teaching. Remember to email, call and go knocking on doors after you have made connections. Door to door job hunting has worked for ages. It worked for Marco and Martin, it worked for your grandpa and it will work for you!

I've been teaching in Japan for one year

If you've been teaching for a bit and still don't have that qualification, **now is the time you need to get a TEFL qualification** and get a better job. After getting his TEFL Charlie immediately got better jobs with higher pay, so it's really in your best interest to get one ASAP.

Be sure to read the section of the book about TEFL, and also check our resources page at **liveworkplayjapan.com/teach-english** for more information about how it will help you.

You might also feel like you are in the position where you are looking to transition away from Japan or English teaching. If it isn't working out for you, remember that Japan has a lot more to offer than just the job you are doing now. There are a lot of ways to live here and English teaching is just one way to pay the bills. Be sure to check our website regularly as we post more information for successful people in Japan, not just in English teaching. While we recommend that you learn Japanese for the undeniable benefits for living here, if you don't there are still a large number of options for you without needing to learn how to speak the language.

I've been here for three years now

If you haven't got that TEFL qualification or higher by now, you're missing out on opportunities. Get it or start looking at the next steps like a CELTA, a Master's degree or further so you can start getting those cushy university teaching jobs with the great pay.

At this point you can start using the network you have been building to start finding other opportunities. Be aware that doing anything outside of teaching or English related services may require a change of visa, which may be easy or hard depending on what you want to change to and where you come from. Unfortunately the easiest way to work in whatever field you like in Japan is still to marry a Japanese person, which may or may not be an option or choice you are able or willing to take. We are still hoping that regulations on the visa in Japan will relax as a greater number of young people are required to fill the gap of this ageing population, but until then you need to keep in mind what your visa status allows.

The permanent residence visa rules are being relaxed a bit more to allow high earners and highly qualified people to get a permanent residency visa more quickly, but for the majority of English teachers this will not affect your chances. The criteria are available on the internet, and it is a point based system. Teaching English affords very few points, and you'll need to be making over ¥4m to even get a few points towards the PR visa, with Master's degrees and doctorates also affording points. If you came to Japan to teach straight after your bachelor's, don't expect to fare well on this front.

If English teaching isn't working for you anymore, now

would be a good time to start transitioning to part-time while you find other opportunities. If you have other relevant skills there are opportunities for you here whether you speak Japanese or not, so don't be afraid to look for a job in marketing if you have marketing experience or a degree, of software development if you are a software engineer. Just go to a Tokyo developer meetup and you'll meet dozens of people not teaching English who are working in Japan without speaking Japanese.

After 5 years, what do I do?

After five years you have invested a lot of time into Japan. If you don't already, now would be a time to get a Master's degree or other qualification, get into some of those business opportunities or think about what you might want to do next. I've met a lot of bitter foreigners in Japan who got stuck getting low pay teaching at eikaiwa or ALT work but can't leave Japan because they have spent years teaching kids and have no idea how to sell their skills. Others may have a new family in Japan to support, and quitting their job or trying something new may feel too risky for them at this point.

Many people also feel that leaving Japan can be career suicide, as employers outside Japan will look down on their English teaching experience. I've heard people characterise it with the phrase, *"Oh, so you played with kids for five years?"*

Of course if you don't prepare for life outside Japan, you may get a less-than-favourable response. If you are smart, you'll have spent your last months (or years) in Japan setting yourself up for success outside of English teaching and outside of Japan. This is really just personal marketing, a skill that we all must learn in the information age. Many people learn to sell the skills they built teaching to get great jobs back home, and the transition to full time teaching in another country is also on the table.

If you're staying for good, set yourself up to get a higher paying and more scaleable job that can give you what you need to raise a family and/or live the life you want here. Look through our techniques for getting higher paying jobs and start looking to the long term. Where do you want to be in another five years? Do you want to start your own business or school? This is a question that you must answer for yourself.

Thank You

Making it in Japan is tough. If you've read this book to the end, you know that people like us don't give up. Whether we are in our hometown or in a country completely foreign to us, we strive to build a better life for ourselves and others. So Martin and Charlie would like to thank you for reading through to the end.

We poured hundreds of hours into writing this book, and years of our experience, trials, failures and successes went into making it available to you. Some of the pitfalls in Japan can be avoided, and we wanted to give you a roadmap to guide you away from the landmines and towards the path to success.

This book is based on our experience and research, but we don't know everything there is to know. The world changes all the time, and we can't promise that everything we talked about here will work ten years from now. We believe that if you apply what we have been teaching here, you'll see a sharp increase in your ability to get rewarding and impactful work in Japan that pays you what you deserve to make. It will require real work, and you will likely fail many times before you succeed. But when you do find a job that suits you, it will be worth the journey.

Resources

All of the resources in this book plus many more are at liveworkplayjapan.com/teach-english

Jobs

www.reddit.com/r/teachinginjapan

Teaching in Japan is a subreddit Diego moderates with nearly 2,000 members at the time of publishing this book. Most of whom are current teachers, living and working in Japan in all areas. Some of them have started their own schools and post at length about how to do this yourself. It's an excellent community to share advice, get tips, lean on the combined experience of the community, and learn to manage your career trajectory.

https://www.reddit.com/r/teachinginjapan/wiki/organizations

This wiki page for the Teaching in Japan subreddit lists every major and most minor organizations that teachers can join in Japan (as well as several throughout Asia). Find the right organizations for yourself and become a member. Having an institution behind you can help build your credibility and expand your resources.

JALT Job Listings

A service provided by the Japan Association for Language Teaching, the largest foreign teacher organization in Japan (though not exclusively for foreign teachers), this is one of the premier resources for finding university job listings.

While not updated frequently, the positions posted are typically high tier.

JALT

The Japan Association for Language Teaching is the largest organization of its kind in Japan. Their annual international conference is the largest language teaching conference in Asia. They have chapters across the country, each with their own events, so find your local chapter and begin to attend meetings to make a name for yourself.

jREC-IN

The other premier source of university job listings, jREC-IN is updated frequently and is used by all major universities. An indispensable resource when searching for university positions. If you are not fluent in reading and writing kanji, make sure you select the "English" option, or you'll be shown the Japanese advertisements meant for fluent Japanese speakers.

Google Chrome

I've used Safari, Firefox, Edge, Opera, and others. They each have their positive attributes, but none make Japanese-English translations as easy to use as Google Chrome. It will come in handy when navigating Japanese university websites or searching online directories. Translations are automated and can be turned off at your request.

IFTTT

If This Then That creates simple command chains that will automatically search for conditions. I use the Craigslist applet to receive an email notification whenever a job or volunteer position is posted that meets my personal search criteria. This helps me get through the clutter and spam ads and save me the time of checking every week for new openings.

We wrote a whole article about how to use IFTTT with Craigslist at Live Work Play Japan, so be sure to check that out to automate this part of your job search.

Distill Web Monitor

Available for Chrome and Firefox, Distill will monitor websites you register in the software and ping you whenever the websites updates. I use it to monitor the vacancy pages for several international schools and some hiring websites. Whenever a positions opens up and the vacancy page is updated, I'll receive a pop-up on my computer or an email if I am away. This means my resume will be one of the first seen.

Japan Student Services Organization

They have compiled a thorough list of all English-language undergraduate and graduate programs in Japan, along with application requirements and important dates.

Japan Association of College English Teachers

Smaller than JALT, JACET is an organization specifically for college English teachers. A good organization to join, attending their conferences/seminars will be an excellent networking opportunity, plus a chance to improve your teaching skills.

Japanese Bilingual Jobs in Japan

https://www.daijob.com/en/

https://www.careercross.com/en

http://www.baitoru.com/lp/foreigner

https://www.hellowork.go.jp

https://tokyo.craigslist.jp

Japanese Recruitment Sites

https://doda.jp/

http://jp.recruit.net/

https://next.rikunabi.com/

https://www.bizreach.jp/

Learning Japanese

"Genki" by Japan Times, "Minna No Nihongo"

These textbook series are very similar. Each covers from 初級日本語 *Shokyu Nihongo* Elementary Japanese to 中級日本語 *Chukyu Nihongo* Intermediate Japanese. Incredibly popular, but also overrated and not fit for the task of learning to **communicate** in Japanese. For that you should use Glossika or JapanesePod101.

"An Integrated Approach to Intermediate Japanese" by Japan Times, "Tobira"

These will prepare you for around the JLPT level 3 and partway through level 2, and is a help for people trying to get from intermediate to advanced (the hardest jump in learning Japanese).

Yookoso!

This series makes an excellent refresher. It is incredibly detailed and indepth. It goes all the way from JLPT level 5 to JLPT level 3 or 2. Jumping from Genki or Minna No Nihongo to the intermediate Japanese books is pretty much impossible. There is too much of a gap. Reviewing with Yookoso! is one way you could manage it. Most teachers find this book too detailed to use for group study. It is best suited for individual study possibly with the help of a tutor or language exchange partner.

JLPT Preparatory Books

The Japanese Language Proficiency Test is a standardized test by the **Japan Foundation**. In Japanese, 日本語能力試験 Nihongo Nouryoku Shiken. While the textbooks above are all somewhat designed to prepare you for this test, that is not their only purpose. From about a level 2 of this test, you can start to use the certificate on your resume to get jobs that require Japanese language ability. By level 2, you are more than elide for many of the bilingual jobs mentioned in this book.

Tae Kim

You can practically learn all the way up to JLPT level 3 or 2 just with this online free grammar tutorial alone. Tae Kim did an amazing job with his grammar guide. The explanations are easy to understand and full of example sentences. No one should study Japanese without referencing this blog. It is that good.

Nihongo Shark

Nihongo Shark is run by Niko who taught English in Japan. He self-taught Japanese during his stay, and later partnered with a local Japanese editor and began English writing, editing and translation work for him. As he traveled around Japan and South East Asia, Niko also began blogging about how to learn Japanese. Over time he has compiled several very easy to follow courses aimed at beginners. From how to learn to read kana and kanji to how to get started with Japanese, check out his free course for beginners: How To Learn Japanese In One Year. How to Start. How to Study. How to Ninja.

*Bonus: If you join Nihongo Shark's course, you can also become a member of a Slack community all working together to master Japanese. Check our page on liveworkplayjapan.com/teach-english for links to the courses we recommend.

Language Exchange

hello-sensei.com/en/sensei

Language exchange site, which you can use to find Japanese teachers. If you want, you can find private students for your English classes or language exchanges. Excellent if you speak other languages like Spanish, Mandarin and French. You can charge more than English teachers sometimes because these languages are in demand but supply of teachers is lower.

www.italki.com

Although italki is meant to be a site to register as a teacher or student for online only classes, this is a great place to meet language enthusiasts in Japan. You can set up language exchanges in person on the site. Just like the sites above, this can be another place to find private students.

国際交流会 *Kokusai Kouryuu Kai* - International Parties

International groups on **Meetup.com** - do a search, there are a lot of them.

www.internationalparty.com - Kokusaika. Regular events for people to meet international people. Has been popular with locals and expats alike for more than a decade.

English.gaitomo.com

cosmobridge.jp/home

Made in the USA
Lexington, KY
10 October 2017